Further Reading

H.W. Dickinson & R. Jenkins, *James Watt and the Steam Engine* (Oxford: Clarendon Press, 1927).

Richard L. Hills, *James Watt, Volume 1: His Time in Scotland, 1736-1774* (Ashbourne: Landmark Publishing, 2002).

Richard L. Hills, *James Watt, Volume 2: The Years of Toil, 1775-1785* (Ashbourne: Landmark Publishing, 2005).

Richard L. Hills, *James Watt, Volume 3: Triumph through Adversity, 1785-1819* (Ashbourne: Landmark Publishing, 2006).

David K. Hulse, *Mechanical Wonders: The Engines that Changed the World* (Stone: David Kenneth Hulse, 2018).

Peter M. Jones, *Industrial Enlightenment* (Manchester: Manchester University Press, 2008).

Christine MacLeod, *Heroes of Invention: Technology, Liberalism and British Identity 1750-1914* (Cambridge: Cambridge University Press, 2007).

Ben Marsden, *Watt's Perfect Engine: Steam and the Age of Invention* (Royston: Icon Books, 2004).

Shena Mason (ed.), *Matthew Boulton: Selling What All the World Desires* (London: Birmingham City Council and Yale University Press, 2009).

Shena Mason, *Soho House Guide* (Birmingham: Birmingham Museums, 2002).

David Philip Miller, *James Watt, Chemist: Understanding the Origins of the Steam Age* (Abingdon: Routledge, 2009).

David Philip Miller, *The Life and Legend of James Watt* (Pittsburgh: Pittsburgh University Press, 2019).

Eric Robinson and A. E. Musson, *James Watt and the Steam Revolution: A Documentary History* (London: Adams & Dart, 1969).

Ben Russell, *James Watt Making the World Anew* (London: Reaktion Books, 2014).

Robert E. Schofield, *The Lunar Society of Birmingham: A Social History of Provincial Science and Industry in Eighteenth-Century England* (Oxford: Clarendon Press, 1963).

Samuel Smiles, *Lives of Boulton and Watt* (London: John Murray, 1865).

Sotheby's, *The James Watt Sale, Art & Science – Sale Catalogue* (London: Sotheby's, 2003).

Jenny Uglow, *The Lunar Men: The Friends Who Made the Future* (London: Faber, 2002).

CONTRIBUTORS

Professor Caroline Archer	Professor of Typography, Birmingham City University
Dr Jim Andrew	Retired Engineering Curator, Birmingham Museums Trust
Eleanor Beestin	History Graduate, University of Birmingham
Valerie Boa	Curator, McLean Museum and Art Gallery, Greenock
Ian Broom	Chief Engineer, Crofton Beam Engines, Wiltshire
John Coulson	Records Manager, Crofton Beam Engines, Wiltshire
Dr Kate Croft	PhD Graduate, University of Birmingham
Dr Malcolm Dick	Director, Centre for West Midlands History, University of Birmingham
Angela Edgar	Curator, Heriot-Watt University, Edinburgh
David Hulse	Independent Researcher and Retired Engineer
Professor Frank A. J. L. James	Professor of History of Science, University College London
Professor Gordon Masterton	Chair of Future Infrastructure, University of Edinburgh
Dr Stephen Mullen	Lecturer in History, University of Glasgow
Christopher Olive	History and Politics Graduate, University of Birmingham
Alexandre Parré	Formerly Heritage Liaison and Collection Co-ordinator, Assay Office Birmingham
Gill Poulter	Heritage Director, Dundee Heritage Trust
Nicky Reeves	Curator, Scientific and Medical History Collections, The Hunterian, University of Glasgow
Chris Rice	Museums and Heritage Consultant
Ben Russell	Curator, Mechanical Engineering, Science Museum, London
Caitlin Russell	History Graduate, University of Birmingham
Simon Russell	Director, IDM Media, Birmingham and History Graduate, University of Birmingham
Dr Kristen M. Schranz	PhD Graduate, University of Toronto
Ian Shearer	Chair, The Friends of Kinneil, Bo'ness
Revd Dr Robert Stephen	Rector of the Ecclesiastical Parish of Handsworth, Birmingham
Rose Teanby	Associate of the Royal Photographic Society
Harry Wilkins	History Graduate, University of Birmingham

Science and Industry Museum
Liverpool Road
Manchester
M3 4FP
https://www.scienceandindustrymuseum.org.uk

St Mary's Church
Handsworth
Birmingham
http://www.birminghamchurches.org.uk/churches/st-marys-anglican-parish-church-handsworth/

Thinktank
Millennium Point
Curzon Street
Birmingham
B4 7XG
http://www.birminghammuseums.org.uk/thinktank

Verdant Works, Dundee
West Henderson's Wynd
Dundee
DD1 5BT
https://www.verdantworks.com/

Watt Library
9 Union Street
Greenock
PA16 8JH
http://www.inverclydeheritage.org.uk/

London Museum of Water and Steam
Green Dragon Lane
Brentford
London
TW8 0EN
http://www.waterandsteam.org.uk/our-engines/boulton-and-watt-engine

Magna Science Adventure Centre
Sheffield Road
Templeborough
Rotherham
S60 1DX
https://www.visitmagna.co.uk/science-adventure

McLean Museum and Art Gallery
15 Kelly Street
Greenock
PA16 8JX
Main website
https://www.inverclyde.gov.uk/community-life-and-leisure/museum
James Watt resources
https://www.inverclyde.gov.uk/community-life-and-leisure/museum/museum-collections/james-watt-1736-1819

National Museum of Scotland
Chambers Street
Edinburgh
EH1 1JF
http://www.nms.ac.uk

National Railway Museum
Leeman Road
York
YO26 4XJ
https://www.railwaymuseum.org.uk/

Powerhouse Museum
500 Harris St
Ultimo
NSW 2007
Australia
http://www.powerhousemuseum.com/collection/

Soho House
Soho Avenue (off Soho Road)
Birmingham
B18 5LB
http://www.birminghammuseums.org.uk/soho

Sandfields Pumping Station
Chesterfield Road
Lichfield
https://lichfieldwaterworkstrust.com/

Science Museum London
Exhibition Road
South Kensington
London
SW7 2DD
http://www.sciencemuseum.org.uk/about_us/collections.aspx

Museums, Art Galleries and Heritage Sites

Assay Office Birmingham
1 Moreton Street
Birmingham
B1 3AX
https://theassayoffice.com/

Birmingham Museum and Art Gallery
Birmingham Museum and Art Gallery
Chamberlain Square
Birmingham
B3 3DH
Main website
http://www.birminghammuseums.org.uk/bmag
Online catalogue
http://www.bmagic.org.uk

British Museum
Great Russell Street
London
WC1B 3DG
http://www.britishmuseum.org/research/collection_online/search.aspx

Cornish Mining World Heritage Site
https://www.visitcornwall.com/things-to-do/history-and-heritage/world-heritage-site

Crofton Pumping Station
Crofton
Marlborough
Wiltshire
SN8 3DW
http://www.croftonbeamengines.org

Deutsches Museum (German Museum)
Museumsinsel 1
80538 München
Germany
http://www.deutsches-museum.de/en

Heathfield Park, formerly Heathfield House and Estate
http://www.legacy-wm.org/site-5-james-watt-gate-house.html

Henry Ford Museum
The Henry Ford
20900 Oakwood Blvd
Dearborn
MI 48124-5029
http://www.thehenryford.org/index.aspx

Hunterian Museum and Art Gallery
The Hunterian
University of Glasgow
Gilbert Scott Building
University Avenue
Glasgow G12 8QQ
http://www.huntsearch.gla.ac.uk

Kinneil Museum
Duchess Anne Cottages
Kinneil Estate
Bo'ness
EH51 0PR
http://www.museumsgalleriesscotland.org.uk/member/kinneil-museum

ARCHIVES

Birmingham Archives and Heritage
Wolfson Centre for Archival Research
Library of Birmingham
Centenary Square
Broad Street
Birmingham
B1 2ND
http://www.birmingham.gov.uk/archives

Institution of Mechanical Engineers Archive
Institution of Mechanical Engineers
1 Birdcage Walk
London
SW1H 9JJ
United Kingdom
http://www.imeche.org/knowledge/library/archive

Sandwell Archives
Smethwick Library
High Street
Smethwick
B66 1AA
http://blackcountryhistory.org

University of Glasgow Archives
13 Thurso Street
Glasgow
G11 6PE
https://www.gla.ac.uk/myglasgow/archives/

1776	The first working Boulton & Watt engine, installed at Bloomfield Colliery, Tipton
	Married Ann McGregor
1777	First engine installed at Cornwall
	Birth of son, Gregory
1779	Birth of daughter, Janet (Jessy)
1780	Patent granted for copying machine
1783	Britain acknowledged sovereignty of the United States of America, ending the American War of Independence
1784	Elected Fellow of the Royal Society of Edinburgh
1785	Elected Fellow of Royal Society of London
1786	First rotative engine installed in a textile mill in Nottinghamshire
1789	Outbreak of French Revolution
1790	Moved to Heathfield House, Handsworth
1794	Death of Jessy Watt
1796	Opening of Soho Foundry, Smethwick, to manufacture steam engines
	Death of Margaret Watt Millar (eldest daughter)
1800	End of Boulton & Watt partnership. Matthew Robinson Boulton and James Watt junior take over the business
1803	Start of the Napoleonic Wars
1804	Death of Gregory Watt
1809	Death of Matthew Boulton
1814	Bust carved by Sir Francis Leggatt Chantrey
1815	Battle of Waterloo, bringing an end to the Napoleonic Wars
1819	James Watt died 25 August and was buried in St Mary's Church, Handsworth

TIMELINE

1736	James Watt born in Greenock, Scotland, to James Watt and Agnes Muirhead
1745-6	Jacobite Rising in which his father's workshop was searched
1753	Watt moved to Glasgow after his mother's death
1755	Watt moved to London to learn the trade of a mathematical instrument maker
1756	Returned to Glasgow
	Watt invited to restore astronomical instruments at Glasgow University
1757	Set up a workshop at Glasgow University
1759	Formed partnership with John Craig to make and sell mathematical instruments
1763-4	Repaired Newcomen engine model at Glasgow University
1764	Married Margaret (Peggy) Miller
1765	Birth of son, John (died late 1765)
	Conceived idea for separate condenser
	Began working with the industrialist John Roebuck to develop experimental steam engine
1767	Formed surveying partnership with Robert Mackell
	Met Dr William Small at Soho Manufactory, Handsworth, near Birmingham
	Birth of daughter, Margaret
	Formed partnership with Roebuck
1768	Applied for steam engine patent
	Met Matthew Boulton in Birmingham
1769	Patent granted for separate condenser
	Birth of son, James junior
	Trials started on experimental engine at Kinneil
1770	Birth of daughter, Agnes (died in 1772)
1773	Roebuck assigned his share of patent to Boulton
	Death of Peggy Watt in childbirth
1774	Moved to Birmingham
1775	Start of the American War of Independence
	Patent for separate condenser extended to 1800
	Went into partnership with Boulton

ACKNOWLEDGEMENTS

Malcolm Dick and Kate Croft, Editors

Our book, *The Power to Change the World: James Watt (1736-1819) – a Life in 50 Objects*, explores the famous man in new ways at a fortuitous time - the 200th anniversary of his death in 1819. Instead of a narrative history, we have selected images of places, people and things to illuminate his life, times and legacy. These are accompanied by articles which explain how these objects cast light on Watt, where he lived, what he made, relationships with family, friends and workers and how he has been remembered.

A major problem was one of selection: which objects do we include and what should we leave out? The editors were assisted by support and enthusiasm for the project from academics, students, curators, archivists, librarians and independent scholars in the United Kingdom and elsewhere. Many of these individuals wrote text to accompany the objects, assisted in supplying high-resolution illustrations which were suitable for publication, and provided copyright permissions to use them.

Several institutions have been crucial in enabling a speedy completion of the manuscript by providing images: Birmingham Assay Office; Birmingham Museums Trust; Dundee Heritage Trust; Falkirk Archives; The Friends of Kinneil; Heriot-Watt University, Edinburgh; The Hunterian, University of Glasgow; Kennet & Avon Canal Trust; Library of Birmingham; Low Parks Museum, Hamilton; McLean Museum and Art Gallery, Greenock; The Mitchell Library, Glasgow; National Galleries of Scotland; Science Museum, London; Science and Society Picture Library. A small number of pictures were obtained from private collections of photographs and prints.

Janet Sullivan has been a characteristically resourceful and efficient picture editor and has been fully involved in assisting the project from conception to birth. Averil and John Maskew have skilfully designed the publication and enhanced images which required improvement before they could be published. The text was also proofread by David Beattie with his customary expertise and extensive knowledge of the intricacies of the English language. The book originated during a discussion between one of the editors and Mike Gibbs of History West Midlands Ltd. Mike's vision, guidance and support enabled the book to be translated from a plan into a product, much like one of James Watt's inventions.

William Bloye's bronze statue of *Boulton, Watt and Murdock*, 1956. The statue shows, from left to right, Murdock, Boulton and Watt.

Boulton, Watt and Murdock by William Bloye, 1956

Malcolm Dick

The sculptor, William Bloye (1890-1975), designed and cast in bronze this larger-than-life statue of Matthew Boulton (1728-1809), James Watt and William Murdock (1754-1839). Bloye was born in Birmingham and educated at the Municipal School of Art and was the city's most prestigious sculptor for much of the twentieth century. His three low reliefs for the interior of the Hall of Memory in 1925 established his reputation.

The statue was initially conceived by Richard Wheatley, a leather-goods manufacturer who bequeathed a sum of £8,000; additional finance was injected by the City Council. It was unveiled in 1956 on a temporary site on Birmingham's Broad Street, outside what was then the Register Office, where it remained for over 50 years. Known locally as the 'Golden Boys', the gilded monument has had its critics: its original location, only yards from the furnishing store, Lee Longlands, has led to its mocking description as the 'wallpaper salesmen' or 'carpet sellers'. It is expected to be relocated in front of the Library of Birmingham during 2019, for the 200th anniversary of Watt's death on 25 August 1819.

According to the inscription on the pedestal, *Boulton, Watt and Murdock* commemorates 'the immense contribution made by Boulton, Watt and Murdock to the industry of Birmingham and the World'. The three men are discussing Watt's diagrams for a steam engine: Boulton the businessman financed its manufacture, whilst Murdock, the skilled worker, helped to translate ideas into reality. Unlike most statues of 'great men', it commemorates, as Sally Hoban has written, 'the collective nature of their industrial achievements', rather than a single figure in isolation. Watt's steam engine improvements were not developed solely by one person, but by other individuals as well in both Scotland and England. In order to do justice to the reality of invention and innovation, a large number of people should have been depicted, but this would, of course, have been difficult and costly. Nevertheless, the 'conversation piece', which portrays a dynamic interaction between the three men, demonstrates that technological innovation is a co-operative enterprise – an important corrective to the heroic representation of single individuals. Watt was significant, but his achievements were only possible because of other entrepreneurs, inventors and workers.

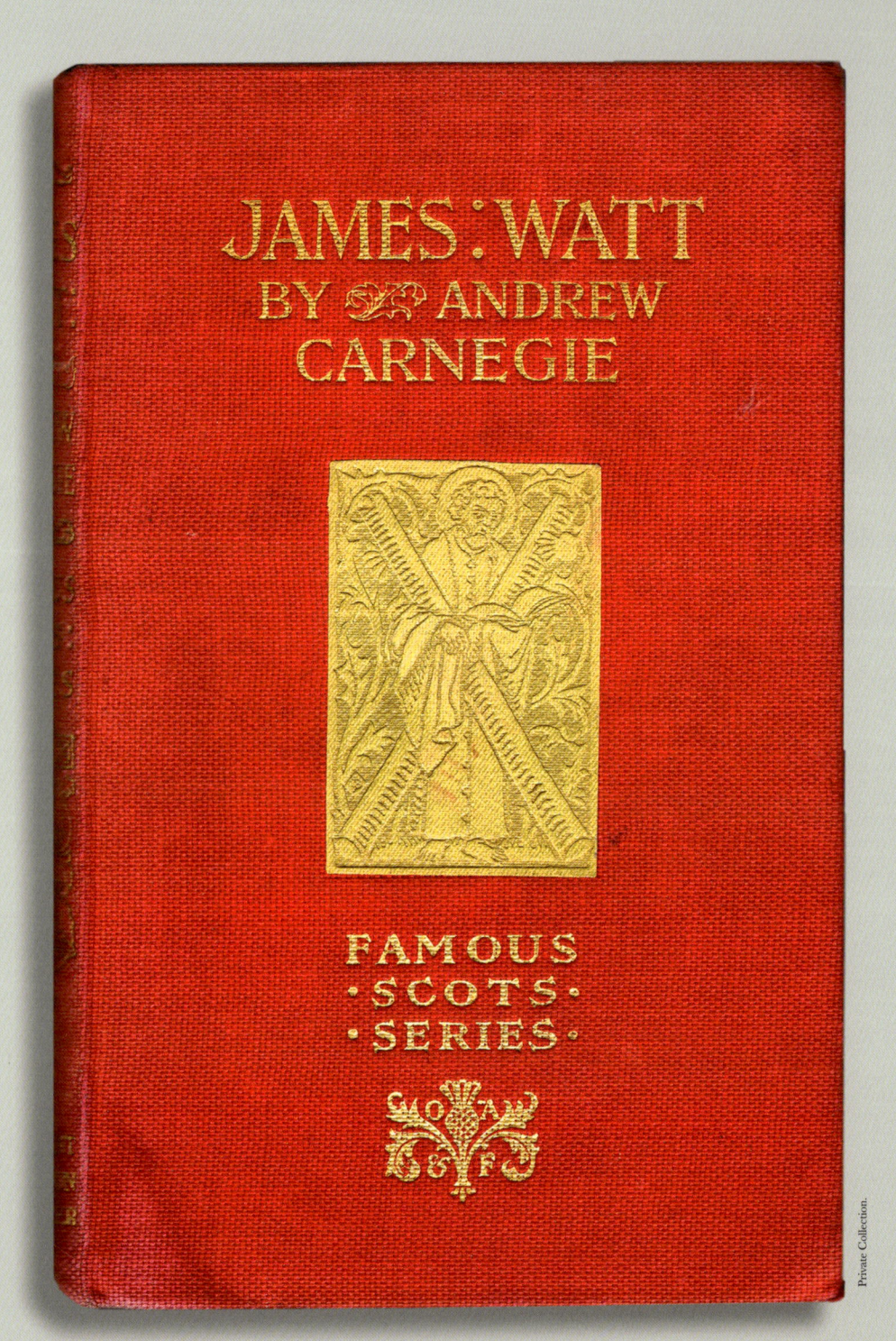

Cover of *James Watt* by Andrew Carnegie, 1905.

Andrew Carnegie's Biography of James Watt, 1905

Ian Shearer

Andrew Carnegie's biography of James Watt was not the first, but is an interesting example of one great individual writing the life of another, which often reveals as much about the biographer, as their subject. Carnegie (1835-1919) was one of the world's wealthiest industrial tycoons and a great philanthropist. Born to a Scottish linen weaver in Dunfermline, his story was one of rags to riches. After the family migrated to the United States in 1848, Carnegie worked hard, rapidly prospered and eventually accumulated a fortune in the steel industry. He saw his own success, like Watt's, as the result of persistence and self-education.

By the end of the nineteenth century, Carnegie was engaged in philanthropy on an astounding scale, most famously by funding libraries for self-improvement across the world. His foundations also supported – as they still do – international peace, research, music and education. The University of Birmingham also benefited: Joseph Chamberlain (1836-1914) negotiated £50,000 from Carnegie in 1900. Carnegie's striking dictum in *The Gospel of Wealth* (1889) was 'The man who dies thus rich dies disgraced'. By his death he had donated $350 million to philanthropic causes. The centenary of Carnegie's death in August 2019 coincides with Watt's bicentenary in the same month and offers an opportunity to reappraise Carnegie as a businessman, philanthropist and Scot.

In his biography of Watt, published in Edinburgh by Oliphant, Anderson and Ferrier in their elegant 'Famous Scots Series', Carnegie unashamedly treats his subject as a hero and reveres the inventor as 'one of the finest characters that ever graced the earth'. It followed earlier examples of Watt 'hagiographies' by Muirhead and Smiles. Carnegie identified with Watt as a paragon of Scottish family upbringing and virtues, and exemplar of the self-made man. Watt, he said, made his own industrial wealth possible: 'Why shouldn't I write the life of the maker of the steam engine, out of which I had made fortune?' It was 'the greatest of all inventions'. The book gleams with pithy, positive observations on Watt's background, character, friends, abilities, business and practices. 'This was a man', Carnegie stirringly concludes. His biography of Watt is an important example of how Watt's reputation continued to be celebrated in the twentieth century.

National Galleries of Scotland.

James Watt and the Steam Engine - The Dawn of the Nineteenth Century by James Eckford Lauder, 1855. Oil painting.

The Dawn of the Nineteenth Century by James Eckford Lauder, 1855

Malcolm Dick

This painting by James Eckford Lauder (1811-1869) was produced when the cult of James Watt was at its height, following the activities of James Watt junior (1769-1848) to promote his father's reputation in medals, statues and books. 1854 saw the founding of the Watt Club following the unveiling of a statue by Peter Slater outside the Watt Institution and School of Arts in Edinburgh (later Heriot-Watt University). The Club, which remains active, listed as one of its purposes 'to sup together on the anniversary of the birth of James Watt'. In the same year, James Patrick Muirhead (1813-1898) published *The Mechanical Inventions of James Watt* in three volumes. As an educated Edinburgh resident, Lauder would have been aware of Watt's importance.

The canvas imagines a moment in 1765 when Watt repaired Glasgow University's model Newcomen engine and realised that the machine's condensation of steam wasted heat – an insight which led him to invent the separate condenser. Watt's gaze is bathed in light, similar in effect to paintings by Joseph Wright of Derby (1734-1797), which also celebrated the wonders of science and technology. Lauder's title *James Watt and the Steam Engine – The Dawn of the Nineteenth Century*, asserts that Watt gave birth to the modern world, when he discovered how to improve the power of steam.

The historian David P. Miller argues that the painting 'captures marvellously the range of representations of Watt that were constructed in the nineteenth century'. As well as illuminating him as a scientific saint, there are other intriguing features in the image. Behind the model, there is, it seems, a kettle on a stove, the household object which, allegedly, began his boyhood experiments with steam. The tools on the table beneath Watt's right hand recognise that he was a mechanic, while the technical diagram and dividers on the left pinpoint his skills as a draughtsman and mathematician. The Scottish engineer Macquorn Rankine (1820-1872) described the Newcomen model on the right as 'a small and uncouth mass of wood and metal', which nevertheless 'shines with imperishable beauty, as the earliest embodiment of the genius of James Watt'. The painting, which was also reproduced as a black-and-white engraving, further communicated Watt's importance as an icon of invention.

James Watt commemorative medal in gold by Joseph S. Wyon, 1858.

Commemorative Medals

Alexandre Parré

Since his death the achievements of James Watt have been commemorated in a series of medals, most of which can be found in the Assay Office Birmingham Private Collection. Produced by a succession of eminent designers and engravers these medals immortalise in metal the life and work of Watt.

One was commissioned by the Watt Club, Greenock and engraved by H. Kirkwood. It depicts a bare-headed Watt and the legend 'Observare' (observe). There was further praise from J. Marrian whose fine engraving depicts a wreath of laurels and the words 'In Testimony of National Esteem'. Issued by Messrs. Thomason and Jones, it expresses the widely-felt approbation for Watt, his importance and legacy; on the reverse it depicts Watt's head and his titles. Other medals celebrate the inventions rather than the man. George Mills created a detailed engraved medal of Watt's steam engine, which also recognised Watt's role as a Fellow of the Royal Society (Science).

Joseph Shepherd Wyon (1836-1873) was the most prolific of Watt's memorial engravers. His first medal is particularly impressive, depicting Watt's steam engine in great detail and high relief. A second, simpler medal merely mentions Watt's dates and the steam engine. Another version of this medal, engraved by Wyon for the Institute of Civil Engineers and issued as an annual prize for papers on mechanical engineering, was first awarded in 1858.

Several medal engravings were based on the statues of Francis Leggatt Chantrey (1781-1841), which depicted Watt seated with plans and divider. One example is found on an unattributed medal praising Watt's qualities 'Ingenio et Labore' (by natural genius and hard work). Matthew Boulton (1728-1809) and Watt were jointly commemorated on a medal engraved by J. Moore. Issued in 1871, it shows their heads conjoined, their common legacy intrinsically linked to each other's success.

Collectively the medals are commemorative tributes to Watt's talents, perseverance and importance as a contributor to human betterment and progress.

James Watt and the Kettle, by Kawanabe Kyōsai, 1873. Japanese woodblock print.

JAMES WATT'S KETTLE

Kate Croft

James Watt and the kettle are synonymous. The image of a young Watt, observing the family's tea-kettle and thus pondering the power of steam has become a useful way of illustrating Watt's youthful curiosity, his early scientific genius and the start of the Industrial Revolution.

The story of James Watt and his kettle appeared in one of the first biographies, written by François Arago (1786-1853). Published in 1830, Arago's *Eloge* included an anecdote related to him by James Watt junior (1769-1848), which originated from Mrs Marion Campbell, a cousin of Watt. According to Mrs Campbell, as a child, Watt had been found holding a plate above a kettle's spout. It did not take long for visual representations of this scene to appear. In 1845 Robert W. Buss's painting, *Watt's First Experiment in Steam* was exhibited at the Royal Academy. In 1863 Marcus Stone's *Watt Discovers the Condensation of Steam* became a popular depiction of the young Watt at home in Greenock, holding a spoon up to a kettle's spout.

Later biographers, such as Samuel Smiles and H. W. Dickinson, dismissed the tea-kettle anecdote as myth, preferring the notion of Watt as an industrious and diligent craftsman rather than inspired genius. However, evidence from Watt's own notebooks supports the tea-kettle anecdote. In these, Watt recorded experiments undertaken 'prior to 1765' in which he used a glass tube and kettle to observe condensing steam and later in 1781, when he again used a kettle to investigate latent heat. The idea of Watt and his kettle has become ubiquitous; it has been continuously illustrated from the nineteenth century onwards, in prints, periodicals, educational texts and popular scientific works. It has been used in marketing campaigns, from collectable cards, to adverts for, inevitably, kettles.

The pervasiveness of the image is best exemplified by a Japanese print, dating from the 1870s, which shows Watt contemplating the kettle, with his aunt looking on. This woodblock print is evidence of the extent of Watt's reputation and influence as an engineer and innovator, reaching an international, non-Western audience, and also of the iconic status of the kettle in the history of Watt, as an emblem of inspiration, progress and the development of steam technology.

Francis Leggatt Chantrey's marble statue, *Monument to James Watt*, in St Mary's Church, Handsworth, 1827.

Monument to James Watt by Francis Chantrey, 1827

Robert Stephen

In his will, James Watt left instructions that when he died he should be 'interred in the most private manner, without show or parade'. His funeral in St Mary's Church, Handsworth, on 2 September 1818 – a week or so after his death on 25 August 1819 – was, however, a public event. James Watt junior (1769-1848), his surviving son, was determined to honour his father further by installing a grand monument above his grave. When he was alive, Watt senior had approved a likeness sculpted by Francis Leggatt Chantrey (1781-1841) and this influenced Watt junior's decision to commission a life-size marble statue of his father. Chantrey was the country's leading sculptor and famous for his moving representation of 'The Sleeping Children' (1817) in Lichfield Cathedral.

The cost of the Watt contract was considerable at £3,500 (over £200,000 in today's money) and Watt junior gave Chantrey a further £500 in appreciation. Carved in 1824–25, it was installed in St Mary's Church in 1827. The pedestal on which it rested was devised by the architect Thomas Rickman (1776-1841), who also designed the Gothic chapel in which the statue rested. The colour of the base and the walls was carefully chosen to complement the marble monument without detracting from it. The cedar wood in the roof above the tracery was strong enough to protect the statue from damage if the tower was to fall down. The thistle in the window – an early attempt at double-glazing in iron – pays tribute to the Scot memorialised in the chapel.

Watt is portrayed deep in thought studying the plans of his improvements to the steam engine. Its calm presence engages the visitor and commemorates the greatness of the man. The architectural historian Nikolaus Pevsner (1902-1983) described the statue as 'a genius left alone with his ideas'. Placing the monument adjacent to the Chancel and close to the High Altar was a statement of the reverence accorded to Watt after his death.

The statue was the first of several Watt monuments which Chantrey created, in Westminster Abbey (1832), the Hunterian Museum, Glasgow University (1833) and Greenock, the town of Watt's birth (1835). In venerating his father, Watt junior combined art and religion to create an icon in marble.

Wellcome Collection. CC BY.

Distinguished Men of Science of Great Britain living in the years 1807-1808, drawn by F. Skill & W. Walker, 1862. Engraving.

The Long Shadow of Watt

Ben Russell

When James Watt died in 1819, he left an immense legacy. The company he helped found in partnership with Matthew Boulton (1728-1809) had built almost 500 steam engines, and in so doing it established new standards and best practices in the emerging field of mechanical engineering.

In the decades that followed, Watt became a new kind of scientific and industrial hero. He was the first engineer to be commemorated in Westminster Abbey, and ascended into Britain's pantheon of national heroes, rubbing shoulders with monarchs, soldiers, sailors and statesmen. The poet William Wordsworth wrote how, 'considering both the magnitude and the universality of his genius', Watt was 'perhaps the most extraordinary man that this country ever produced'. His steam engine was the symbolic machine in what Thomas Carlyle christened the Age of Machinery. The engraving, *Distinguished Men of Science* shows Watt in a prominent position, seated in front of the table. Boulton is to his immediate right.

However, Watt's legacy was not without controversy. Although the engine he conceptualised was of vital significance, many engineers felt stifled in their attempts to create new designs and uses for it. Equally, Boulton and Watt's defence of their patents led to subsequent claims that they held an unfair monopoly: the historian T. S. Ashton wrote how the authority they had was 'sufficient to clog engineering enterprise for a generation'.

In the nineteenth century, the profession of engineering which Watt helped build assumed a pivotal importance to Britain. Steamships of unparalleled size linked together the greatest trading network ever known. Steam locomotives similarly provided the motive power for a rapidly expanding railway system. In some vital ways, these engines were different from Watt's: they were smaller, self-contained and more powerful for their size, employing 'strong steam' – steam at high operating pressure – rather than depending on low pressures and vacuums as Watt's engine did. But, in their gestation and diffusion they owed much to him: here was the engine as a new primal force, ultimately able to cross the widest sea, travel at speeds previously only dreamed of, or pump dry the deepest mine. Watt set a standard to some extent for what *should* be done, but much more for what *could* be done. The engineers who followed utilised new technologies to pursue myriad possibilities that Watt could only have dreamed of.

James Nasmyth's model of James Watt's steam engine, 1825.

Model Steam Engine by James Nasmyth, 1825

Angela Edgar

In 1817 a young boy coming home from school saw a visitor leaving his father's house in Edinburgh. The boy was James Nasmyth (1808-1890), the son of portrait painter Alexander Nasmyth (1758-1840), and he would become one of the foremost engineers of the nineteenth century: the steam hammer was one of his inventions. The visitor was James Watt and Nasmyth later wrote: 'I had just returned from the High School when he was leaving my father's house. It was but a glimpse I had of him but his benevolent countenance and his tall but bent figure made an impression on my mind that I can never forget.'

Eight years later, having left the High School at the age of twelve and studied at the newly established Edinburgh School of Arts for five years, Nasmyth felt that he 'had acquired a considerable amount of practical knowledge as to the use and handling of mechanical tools, and I desired to turn it to some account'. He turned his bedroom into a miniature brass foundry, bricking up the fireplace, taking up the carpet and installing a furnace fuelled by gas coke and cinders from the kitchen. Among other sources of brass used in this foundry were 'a pair of old candlesticks that I begged of my Father'. In time, using his bedroom foundry and the tools in his father's workshop, he 'was able to construct working models of steam engines (including) a sectional model of a complete condensing steam-engine of the beam and parallel motion construction. The model, as seen from one side, exhibited every external detail in full and due action when the flywheel was moved round by hand; while, on the other or sectional side, every detail of the interior was seen, with the steam valves and air pump, as well as the motion of the piston in the cylinder.'

He made a number of these sectional models and sold them to mechanics institutes and other institutions for £10 each, but the first was made for the Edinburgh School of Arts, where he had studied. The Edinburgh School of Arts eventually became Heriot-Watt University and the model is one of the jewels of the University's historic collections.

Steamship *Caledonia* shown with Danish flags by an unknown artist, 1817, MS 3147/5/1243. Hand-coloured print.

THE CALEDONIA, 1817

Simon Russell

In 1807 the American entrepreneur Robert Fulton (1765-1815) ordered a light, compact and powerful steam engine from Boulton & Watt. The engine was for his new boat, *The North River Steamer*, which launched the world's first steamboat service between New York and Albany. Within a decade of Fulton's order Boulton, Watt & Co – despite being based in land-locked Birmingham – had become a leading supplier of steamboat engines. It was a growing market, but with the original patent on Watt's steam engine long-since expired, the company faced increasing competition.

In order to prove their prowess in this new market, Boulton & Watt purchased a ship in 1817 called *The Caledonia* and fitted it with their engines. But *The Caledonia* was much more than a floating advertisement for the firm – it was a laboratory: an opportunity to perfect and develop steamboat technology in a methodical and scientific way. Sea trials for *The Caledonia* were conducted almost exclusively by James Watt junior (1769-1848) who kept meticulous notes throughout the voyage. These notes covered diverse topics, such as the best arrangement for paddle-wheels, coal consumption and performance in rough seas. This scientific work also attracted considerable interest from his father – James Watt senior.

Watt senior had been hesitant to use high-pressure steam technology on the open water and described the steamboat concept as 'impracticable' – but he began to warm to the idea as the market for these engines grew and the firm perfected their application. Often reminding Watt junior of the risks involved, Watt senior nevertheless offered much advice to his son and helped directly with numerous engineering problems. After several cycles of development *The Caledonia* became a celebrated steamship. After winning a race in 1818, an excited Watt junior wrote that *The Caledonia*'s speed was 'superior to any steam vessel that has been made'. With the firm's expertise proved and their technology honed, *The Caledonia* had served its purpose and was sold off in 1819. The ship represents a significant milestone in the history of Boulton & Watt – as they entered the steamboat engine market in a big way, supplying thousands of horsepower to both the Royal Navy and merchant shipping companies.

Flying Horse Imaging / Kennet & Avon Canal Trust.

The Engine House, Crofton, Wiltshire.

Boulton & Watt Engine, Crofton Pumping Station, 1812

Ian Broom and John Coulson

Crofton Pumping Station in Wiltshire dates from 1807-9 and houses two beam pumping engines which provide water to the summit level of the Kennet and Avon Canal. The oldest surviving engine in its original location was bought from Boulton & Watt at a cost of £2040 and was in operation by 1812. It has a 42-inch-diameter cylinder and drives a 30-inch-diameter lift pump but ceased commercial use in 1959. The Station was bought by the Kennet and Avon Canal Trust in 1968 and the engine was restored to full operational use. It is probably the oldest working beam engine in the world doing its original job in its original engine house.

Over the years it has been modified, but can still claim to be a Boulton & Watt engine. In 1844, it was converted to the Cornish Cycle by fitting new double-beat valves, the condenser was moved to the pump side of the beam wall and the parallel motion was modified to suit. New double-beat valves were fitted to the pump and the three Boulton & Watt wagon boilers were replaced by three Cornish boilers working at a much higher pressure. All this work was carried out by Messrs Harvey & Co. of Hayle, Cornwall. In 1896 the engine suffered a major failure – details are not known but the engine was out of action for a year. The cylinder was rebored and it is also clear that parts of the indoor parallel motion are not of standard Boulton & Watt design. A major overhaul of the plant was then undertaken. New Lancashire boilers were installed. New Pernis multi-ring valves were fitted to the pump and the whole of the well structure strengthened.

Following restoration the engine was restarted on 4 April 1970 and has continued to run on a regular basis since then without any major incidents. Indeed, it has been called into action to keep the Canal operational when the regular electric pumps fail. A major programme of work, largely financed by the Heritage Lottery Fund, was carried out in 2018-2019 to preserve and enhance the site so that the engines can continue to be demonstrated on regular steaming weekends throughout the summer months.

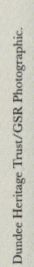

The Douglasfield Engine, Verdant Works Museum, Dundee.

DOUGLASFIELD BOULTON & WATT ENGINE, DUNDEE

Gill Poulter

The Douglasfield Engine is one of only four surviving rotative engines by Boulton & Watt in the United Kingdom. It is the only surviving Watt engine that worked in Scotland and the only one that remains close to its original place of working. The engine was used to turn machinery at William Sandeman's Douglasfield Bleachworks, located on the Dighty Burn just outside Dundee. At the beginning of the nineteenth century Douglasfield had the lion's share of Dundee's bleaching trade, an important element of the thriving local linen industry. Costing £517, the engine was ordered from Boulton & Watt in February 1801 and was installed at the bleachworks in March 1802. Sandeman soon sent word back to the makers that 'his engine gave perfect satisfaction'. Little is known of the engine's working history after this but it is believed it continued to operate for most of the century.

In 1898 the engine was purchased and gifted to the Free Library Committee, responsible for Dundee's museum at the time, 'through the munificent generosity of a few citizens'. It was too large to be displayed in the Albert Institute (now The McManus, Dundee's Art Gallery and Museum) so a separate Technical Museum was established. Opening in 1900 the engine continued to be displayed there until 1939 when the building was requisitioned for war work and the museum closed, never to re-open.

Press comment in the late 1940s illustrated some negative opinions about the industrial museum, including 'a lot of old stuff that no-one cared about' and 'the engine took up a good deal of space and should be scrapped'. Fortunately this never happened and it was dismantled and placed in store, where it remained for over sixty years. In 2012 Dundee Heritage Trust began working in partnership with the engine's owner Dundee City Council and Leisure & Culture Dundee, who care for it on their behalf, on an ambitious scheme to conserve the engine. The project, supported by the Heritage Lottery Fund, Museums Galleries Scotland and the Association for Industrial Archaeology, saw an expert professional team come together to restore this magnificent engine to working order (via electric motor) and put it on public display within the stunning High Mill at Verdant Works.

Brace and bits presented to the Hart brothers, 1815.

BRACE AND BITS PRESENTED TO JOHN AND ROBERT HART, 1815

Valerie Boa

In 1814 a tall, elderly gentleman entered the shop in Glasgow where brothers Robert and John Hart were working. He was accompanied by one of their employers, Miss McGregor, who asked them to show him a small engine they had made. The gentleman examined it and asked pertinent questions. John was pointing out elements of Watt's design when Miss McGregor responded: 'Oh, he understands it; this is Mr Watt.' They then explained their ideas for improving the engine and Watt reciprocated with reminiscences about his own experiments. He remarked that one of their practical tricks to make temporary steam joints on engines put him in mind of his younger days. The Harts were invited to Miss McGregor's house where they discussed the new technologies of the time. John asked Watt where the idea for the separate condenser had come to him and Watt related the story of his walk on Glasgow Green where the potential of the separate condenser revealed itself to him.

The details of these encounters were recalled by Robert 43 years later. The meetings also made a lasting impression on Watt as on 19 December 1815 he gifted a presentation set of brace and bits (a brace is a hand tool which holds a bit to drill holes) to the brothers with an accompanying letter sent from his home at Heathfield, near Birmingham:

> On Saturday last I took the liberty of sending by the Manchester waggon for Glasgow a small box, directed as this letter, containing a best Sheffield Brace and 30 bits and two drill stocks, with 12 drills each, of which I request your acceptance as a mark of my regard. I hope they will be of use in your pursuits. They may be at Glasgow in about a fortnight and you may enquire for the box at Mrs Walshe's in Stirling Square – I shall be glad to hear that you receive them safe, and how your telescope goes on and remain with esteem.

The brace and bits are in the collections of the McLean Museum, Greenock. Watt's gift to the brothers is an example of his interest in and support for the work of a younger generation of skilled workers.

Sketch of an oak tree by Gregory Watt, n.d. MS 3219/8/4.

GREGORY WATT (1777-1804)

Harry Wilkins

Gregory Watt was born on 10 October 1777, the eldest child of James Watt and his second wife Ann (1738-1832). Gregory spent his younger years educated by his mother, before spending time at a preparatory school in Birmingham. He kept a diary, in which he wrote about his school days and time spent with his mother. At a young age he became an accomplished artist, creating portraits and paintings of the natural world.

In 1792, at the age of 15, Gregory was sent to Glasgow University. His time there was strongly directed by his father, who in his letters guided Gregory's studies towards chemistry, natural philosophy, arithmetic and writing, as well as history, German and Italian. In his four years at Glasgow he also attended a debating society which discussed topics ranging from classical poetry to contemporary politics. Upon leaving Glasgow in 1796, Gregory joined Boulton & Watt's firm at Soho. By 1797 he was staying in Cornwall for the benefit of his health. While there, however, he acted on his father's behalf, aiding in the logistics of erecting steam engines and reporting on the actions of Boulton & Watt's chief competitor for manufacturing patents, Jonathan Hornblower (1753-1815).

Gregory left Glasgow a skilled and passionate mineralogist. While in Cornwall he stayed in Redruth, the focal point of the Cornish mining industry, completing a geological survey of Cornwall. Throughout his life, Gregory's health troubled him; he often suffered from difficulty breathing and from fevers. He gave up working for Boulton & Watt in 1801, and travelled in Europe, visiting France, Germany, Italy and Austria, to further his geological interests. His letters to his father show his enthusiasm for geological sites and other places of interest. His studious nature stayed with him, as he attended lectures on geology and mineralogy in the places he visited.

As his health deteriorated, Gregory spent his last months in the care of his parents. He moved from Bath to Sidmouth, and then Exeter. He died of consumption in Exeter on 16 October 1804, aged 27. Friends of the Watt family sent many letters of condolence and his brother, James Watt junior (1769-1848), penned moving notes of a biography that seems never to have been completed.

© Birmingham Museums Trust.

Aston Hall, East Front by John Joseph Hughes, 1854. Oil painting.

JAMES WATT JUNIOR (1769-1848)

Malcolm Dick

As James Watt's heir, James Watt junior took over the direction of the Boulton & Watt companies with Matthew Boulton's son, Matthew Robinson Boulton (1770-1842) in the late 1790s when their fathers retired from day-to-day management.

After his schooling, aged 15, James junior was sent to the Bersham Works of John Wilkinson (1728-1808) in North Wales to learn practical business skills. He worked in the carpenter's shop and learned bookkeeping, geometry and algebra. His education was completed on the continent, where he studied the classics, French, history, science, mathematics and drawing and met with scientists. In 1788, he returned to England and in Manchester acted as his father's agent to sell steam engines whilst participating in the intellectual life of the town. James junior welcomed the French Revolution of 1789 and in 1792 he went to Paris with his friend Thomas Cooper (1759-1839), where they met with radicals and presented a supportive address to the extreme revolutionary Jacobin Club. Edmund Burke MP (1729-1797) publicly denounced them as traitors and Watt senior was horrified. As the French Revolution became increasingly violent, however, Watt junior's attitudes changed. He feared being denounced as a spy, fled to Italy and subsequently returned to England in 1794.

Father and son were reconciled and James junior became involved in the business. He brought to court those who had infringed his father's patents, promoted the copying machine and took over the development of the Soho Foundry in Smethwick, the world's first purpose-built mechanical engineering works. In the early nineteenth century, engines manufactured at Soho were purchased to drive machinery, sold to crush sugar cane on Caribbean slave plantations, and procured to power ships. As a result of business success, in 1817 he leased Aston Hall, where he lived until his death in 1848.

James Watt junior not only continued his father's work, he also cemented his legacy. Henry Cavendish (1731-1810) who had questioned Watt's findings on the composition of water was denigrated and medals and sculptures were commissioned which celebrated Watt in metal and marble. He also sponsored complimentary publications by his kinsman James Patrick Muirhead (1813-1898). James Watt junior invested a huge amount of time, energy and money to promote his father's reputation. Positive public perceptions of James Watt since his death in 1819 are substantially due to his son's filial project.

Dining room of Soho House, home of Matthew Boulton.

Dining Table at Soho House, Handsworth, c. 1798

Chris Rice

James Watt was a member of the Lunar Society, an informal group of friends who were natural philosophers or scientists, inventors and writers. The group was so-named because it met on the Monday nearest to the full moon in order to have enough light for its members to make their way home. The Society comprised some of the finest minds of the day. It was jointly founded by the industrialist Matthew Boulton (1728–1809) and the physician Dr Erasmus Darwin (1731-1802) around 1767. Other members included Dr William Small (1734-1775), Joseph Priestley (1733-1804), Josiah Wedgwood (1730-1795), James Keir (1735-1820), John Whitehurst (1713-1788), Samuel Galton junior (1753-1832), Richard Lovell Edgeworth (1744-1817), Thomas Day (1748-1789) and Dr William Withering (1741-1799). The Society met often at Soho House, home of Watt's business partner Matthew Boulton. The group enjoyed a good meal in the dining room, and afterwards discussed subjects, including science.

Boulton had Soho House remodelled and enlarged in the 1790s to the designs of the brothers James (1746-1813) and Samuel Wyatt (1737-1807). Both the exterior and interior of the building were remodelled, with much of the internal joinery being undertaken by Benjamin Wyatt (1775-1852), a cousin of the two architects. Although no definitive documentation exists confirming that the dining table was made by Benjamin, he was responsible for fitting out the Dining Room in 1797/8, which included supplying a significant amount of mahogany. The table's dimensions suggest that it was specifically made for this space, which was quite modest in scale compared with dining rooms in other fashionable houses.

By the time the dining table was made, the Lunar Society was declining. Small, Wedgwood, Whitehurst and Day were dead; Priestley had migrated to America and the surviving members were dispersed around the country. Even so, the Society continued until 1813, and the famous astronomer Sir William Herschel (1738–1822) attended one of the meetings at Soho House in the summer of 1801. The table exudes a powerful sense of place, located as it is in the superbly restored dining room at Soho. It is not difficult to imagine Watt, Boulton and some of the other Lunar Men sitting around it discussing the great questions of the day.

Apprentices Presents Xmas 1800			Apprentices Xmas 1801		
Foundery			**Foundery**		
Joseph Marsh	–	5 –	Joseph Marsh	Premium	
Wm Meadows	–	5 –	Wm Meadows	Do	
Charles Betts	–	5 –	Charles Betts	0	0 0
Thos Withers	–	5 –	Thos Withers	0	0 0
Thos Wells	–	5 –	Thomas Wells	–	5 –
Richd Webster	–	5 –	Richd Webster	–	5 –
Geo Croft	–	5 –	Out of his Apprenticeship		
Saml Walford	–	– –	Samuel Walford	–	5 –
Boys not Bound			James Pearsall	–	5 –
Thos Phillips	–	2 6	Thos Phillips	–	5 –
Barnabas Croft	–	2 6	Barnabas Croft	–	5 –
	£2	– –	Wm Ravenall Junr	–	5 –
			Boys not Bound		
			Wm Mowsley	–	2 6
			Alexr Croft	–	2 6
				£2	– –
Fitters			**Fitters**		
Simeon Allport	–	10 6	Simeon Allport	Harrison	13 –
John Johnson	–	10 6	John Johnson	"	10 6
Francis Taylor	–	5 –	Francis Taylor	"	7 6
			Wm Wells	"	5 –
			John Baker	"	– –
Thos Hunt	–	10 6	Thos Hunt	Bunting	13 –
James Wells	–	5 –	James Wells	W. Wells	6 –
			Benjn Partridge	Bysaker	7 6
	£4	1 6		£5	2 6

John Hughes has been working up here some time
Please say whether he is to have any present
I am going to Birmingham with the lads after Breakfast

List of Christmas presents given to the apprentices at Soho Foundry, late eighteenth/early nineteenth century.
MS 3147/8/43/2-6.

Soho Foundry Apprentices

Caitlin Russell

The Soho Foundry, established in Smethwick in 1796, was where Boulton & Watt's steam engines were made. In the foundry, apprentice boys as young as fourteen years old worked alongside experienced workmen learning the skills of the trade such as 'moulding and casting iron', and 'filing and fitting iron'. The tools and techniques used in the foundry were at the cutting edge of mechanical engineering, and as such the boys were challenged to keep up as the techniques advanced.

Though young boys, they were still employees who had to abide by their employer's rules. Gambling and drinking alcohol were forbidden in an attempt to shape their behaviour and attitudes at work. In the event of those rules being broken, Matthew Boulton (1728-1809) and James Watt, and their successors Matthew Robinson Boulton (1770-1842) and James Watt junior (1769-1848), chose to discipline the unruly behaviour of apprentices, but in a paternalistic way. They used Christmas presents of small amounts of money as rewards and incentives for good behaviour that the boys could then spend as disposable income. This was important as their usual wage served only to cover food and lodging costs. To discipline bad behaviour, the treat of a Christmas present was simply withheld from the boy that year.

Accounts of which boys were to receive presents were written in lists. One list includes a note from James Watt junior saying he would be 'going to Birmingham with the lads after breakfast' to allow them to spend their money if they wanted. This suggests a familiarity with the boys which goes beyond merely seeing them as workers to make profits. Indeed in 1804, when the boys managed to break twenty-two windows between them, each boy's Christmas money was reduced to cover damage costs and to teach them that actions have consequences. To further encourage good behaviour, their weekly wages and Christmas present amounts increased for each year they were good employees. The boys normally completed their apprenticeships once they were 21 years old, and most of them then continued to work for Watt in the foundry, as well-trained and capable mechanical engineers.

Private Collection.

James Watt's chair and lunch basket in Thinktank, Birmingham Museums Trust (toasting fork not illustrated).

Watt at work: a chair, lunch basket and toasting fork

Jim Andrew

Few of James Watt's personal possessions survive but three items do, including a chair from his office, a lunch basket and a toasting fork. All three offer an insight into how humble household objects facilitated his productivity and comfort during his working hours.

During his working life, Watt spent hours composing letters, drafting technical information and producing drawings for his businesses and customers. Eighteenth-century chairs were not always designed for the convenience of the busy businessman or engineer. Watt's chair, with legs offset to the side, was much more stable than an ordinary one, which could topple over when the sitter needed to reach to find documents, drawings and ledgers which were not immediately to hand.

When Watt became engrossed in projects or activities he wished to avoid interruption, even for meals. He had a large workshop in his home at Heathfield Hall, Handsworth, where he could write, invent and develop devices such as his sculpture machines. This lunch basket was simply an object which made his life easier. It was packed with food which was left outside the workshop door by his family or servants so that he had access to food without leaving his workplace.

As well as being an item which enhanced his comfort, the toasting fork is an example of Watt's constant desire to innovate and improve. The traditional toasting fork required the user to sit in front of a hot fire and physically turn the bread over to toast the other side. Watt designed a much-improved version, which supported the bread in two hooked fingers hanging from a swivel. He could sit to the side of the fire, away from direct heat and simply swivel the bread round to toast the other side. While the innovation Watt made to the toasting fork may not be as revolutionary as those he applied to the steam engine, it does reveal Watt actively applying his mind to the small inconveniences of everyday life as well as to the larger engineering and technical challenges, for which he is better known.

© Birmingham Museums Trust.

James Watt's Work Room by Jonathan Pratt, 1889. Oil painting.

Watt's Workshop at Heathfield Hall

Ben Russell

James Watt's workshop is a jewel in the collections of the Science Museum, London. It was acquired in 1924, having been preserved for 105 years since Watt died, and comprises a physical record of his life's work and personal interests.

In the attic of his home at Heathfield, one room was initially used as a store, but Watt slowly converted it into a workshop. Upon his death, Watt left most of his estate to his second wife, Ann (1738-1832), but the workshop was specifically passed to James Watt junior (1769-1848), who kept it locked up until his own death in 1848. Thereafter, visitors included biographers Samuel Smiles and James Patrick Muirhead, and Bennet Woodcroft of London's Patent Office Museum. In the later nineteenth century the workshop was occasionally opened, and its deteriorating state was noted. Only in 1924, with Heathfield on the verge of demolition, was the complete workshop donated to the Science Museum, where it has been displayed ever since.

The workshop played two roles for Watt. First, it was a practical workplace. He had a longstanding interest in sculpture, and devoted himself in retirement to building two sculpture-copying machines, one to make reproductions on a reduced scale, and one for equal-size copies. These two still dominate the workshop, along with components from their early development, many pieces of sculpture, their copies, and the ingredients for reproducing them in plaster.

The workshop's second role was as a personal museum for Watt. It contains objects stretching back to the 1750s when he worked as a scientific and musical instrument maker in Glasgow, and other items document his work as a potter and a chemist. Other objects have more personal associations: chief among these is the chest containing books and writings of Gregory Watt, who tragically died of consumption in 1804, aged 27.

The workshop is a unique portrayal of endeavour during what has been termed Britain's 'Industrial Enlightenment', the heady combination of new ideas and their practical implementation which proved to be so fruitful in the late eighteenth and early nineteenth centuries. It reflects a combination of arts and sciences and a mixture of diverse interests, which remains rare today.

Heathfield Hall by Allen Edward Everitt, 1835. 1977/V/43. Watercolour.

Heathfield Hall, Handsworth

Chris Rice

When he moved to Birmingham in 1774 James Watt lived at New Hall and then Harper's Hill, in what is now the Jewellery Quarter. By 1789 the success of the Boulton & Watt steam engine business meant that he was a wealthy man and could afford to build a new house on the newly enclosed Handsworth Heath, a few miles outside Birmingham. The stucco-clad neo-classical villa was the work of the Staffordshire-born architect Samuel Wyatt (1737-1807). Thanks in part to his friendship with Matthew Boulton (1728-1809), Wyatt had undertaken a number of commissions in and around Birmingham. These included the Theatre Royal (1780), Soho House (1796-9) and Shugborough Hall in Staffordshire (*c.* 1800). He also designed Albion Mills in London for Boulton, the first flour mill in the world to be powered by Boulton & Watt steam engines.

Watt moved into Heathfield in 1790. An inventory made by Ann Watt (1738-1832) in 1791 shows that it was both fashionably and comfortably furnished and featured steam central heating similar to Boulton's at Soho House. The surrounding estate, which was around fifty acres in size, boasted a circular driveway, a lake, shrubberies and tree plantations. In 1800 Watt retired from business but continued to experiment and invent in a garret workshop located over the kitchen at Heathfield. It was there that he developed and perfected his three-dimensional copying machines – often using Sir Francis Chantrey's bust of himself as his template. On Watt's death in 1819, his workshop at Heathfield was locked up and remained undisturbed for over thirty years. It was first reopened in 1853 for Watt's biographer, James Patrick Muirhead. However, a full catalogue of its contents was not made until 1885.

Ann Watt continued to live at Heathfield until her death in 1832. The Watt family leased the estate to the writer Thomas Pemberton in 1857, and then to the engineer George Tangye in 1876 who lived there until his death in 1920. The estate was sold in 1924 and the house demolished in 1927 to make way for a new housing estate. However, the contents of Watt's workshop were preserved in their entirety and presented to the Science Museum in London.

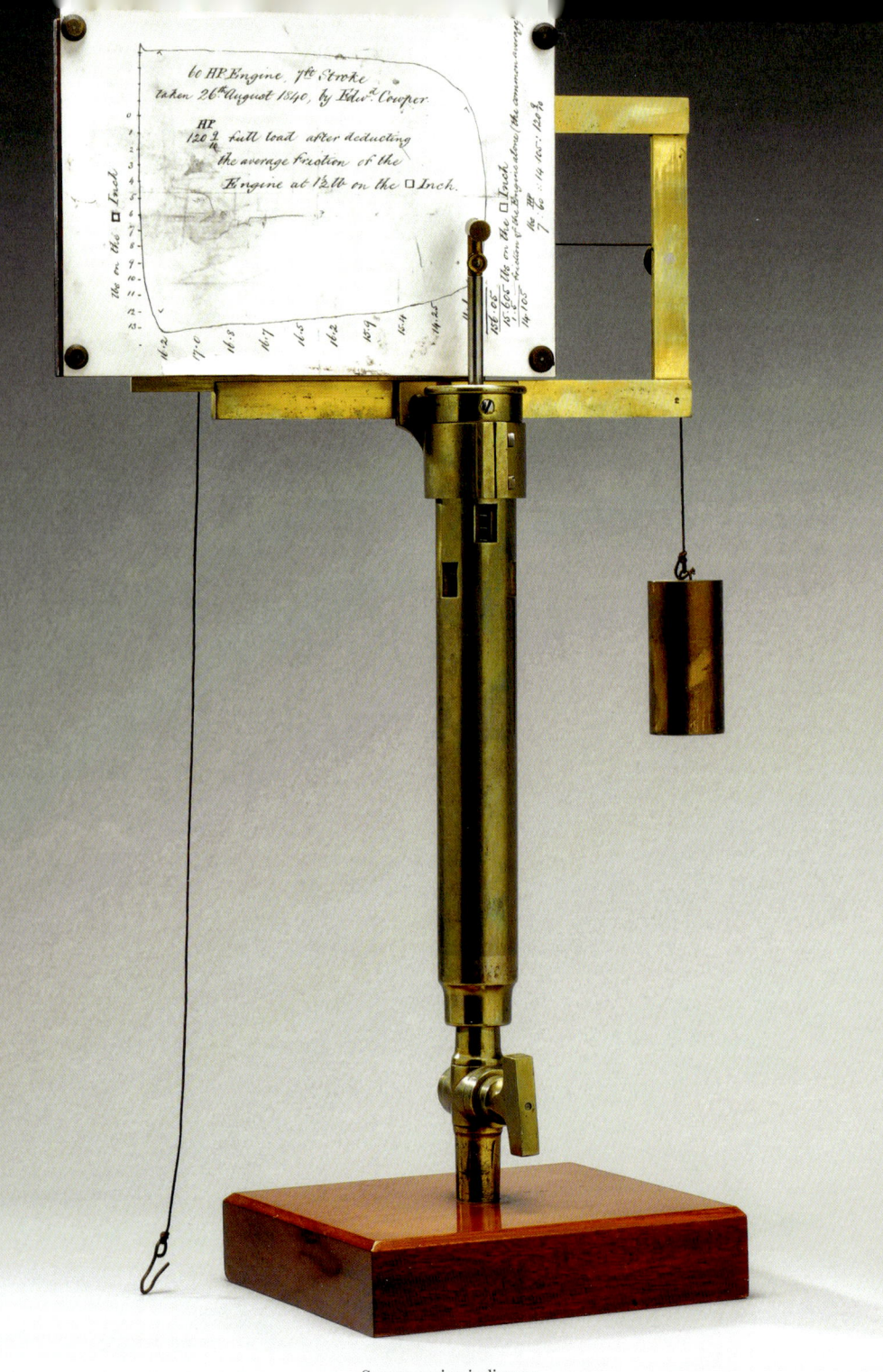

Steam engine indicator.

STEAM ENGINE INDICATOR, 1796

Ben Russell

A vital part of the nineteenth-century steam engineer's toolkit was an engine indicator, an instrument to measure and capture in graphic form what happens to steam during an engine's working cycle. Performing the same role as a doctor's stethoscope, the indicator became a valued diagnostic device. The indicator was not, as is sometimes believed, the personal invention of James Watt. Correspondence inside the company of Boulton & Watt suggests that it was brought into use from around 1796 by Watt's assistant, John Southern (1758-1815). The company issued the instrument to its engine erectors, to assist them in getting newly-built engines up and running smoothly. Such was its value that the indicator's use remained a closely-guarded secret. John Farey, acclaimed chronicler of the steam engine, only saw it in use for the first time in 1819, in Russia.

The indicator had a small cylinder that could be attached to the full-size cylinder on a steam engine. The steam exerted force on a piston within, which in turn was attached to a piston rod with a pencil on top. As the engine went through its operating cycle, the pencil traced the rising pressure and vacuum on a paper-covered tablet, attached to the engine's moving parts so that it moved back and forth. The resulting indicator diagram helped the engineer understand what was happening inside the engine.

As well as being a practical tool, the indicator also hints at modern historical controversy concerning Watt's role as a scientist, and his theories of heat. He became widely regarded in the nineteenth century as a pioneer of thermodynamics, the emerging modern science of heat. However, as conceived in the 1790s, the indicator was used to measure steam's 'strength' or pressure. For Watt, this was the product of the latent heat contained within steam, which provided the elasticity upon which the engine depended to operate. Watt's understanding of latent heat was not of a type of energy, but as a chemical compound. Thus, the indicator was not conceived as the thermodynamic instrument it came to be regarded as, but we can instead view it as a piece of chemical apparatus.

Optics equipment in James Watt's workshop, Science Museum.

Watt's Experiments in Optics

Rose Teanby

James Watt died before the beginnings of photography were revealed by William Henry Fox Talbot (1800-1877) and Louis-Jacques-Mandé Daguerre (1787-1851) in 1839. Watt, however, appears to have had a long-standing fascination with visual recording and the study of optics. His portable Perspective Drawing Machine (1765) shows his interest in accurate pictorial representation. It was based on an easel which used a pantograph – a jointed framework – to enable an artist to trace an object. For centuries, another device, the *camera obscura* was used as a drawing aid. The *camera obscura* (Latin for darkened room) is a box which creates a precise optical image of a subject. It makes use of a natural optical phenomenon where light rays pass through a lens and come to a focus upside down on a screen opposite. The first photographic cameras in the nineteenth century used this phenomenon to make a permanent image on a surface covered with light-sensitive material such as silver salts.

Given that Watt's library contained William Emerson's *The Elements of Optics: in Four Books* (1768), it is not surprising that his Heathfield workshop, now in the Science Museum, contains a quantity of optical glass, and a hand mill for the preparation of lenses. A wooden box in the workshop, labelled *Camera and other Glasses, focus and mirrors*, houses a rectangle of silvered glass, beneath a square of ground glass, two components of a *camera obscura*. Elsewhere, there were two flint-glass lenses, mounted on pasteboard. An inventory of the workshop appeared in Samuel Smiles' *Lives of the Engineers; Boulton and Watt* (1865). Smiles commented: 'An extemporised camera with the lenses mounted on pasteboard, and many camera-glasses laid about, indicate interrupted experiments in optics.'

Communication between Watt and Josiah Wedgwood II (1769-1843) has constantly given rise to speculation about their interest in the subject and Humphry Davy (1778-1829), the chemist and inventor, reported at the Royal Institution in 1802 that Josiah's brother Thomas (1771-1805) conducted early photographic experiments involving the reaction of silver nitrate within a *camera obscura*. A letter from Watt to Wedgwood in 1799 begins, 'Dear Sir, I thank you for your directions for the silver pictures, on which when at home I shall try some experiments.'

Thomas Beddoes after E. Bird. Undated. Pencil drawing.

JAMES WATT AND THOMAS BEDDOES (1760-1808)

Frank A. J. L. James

In the mid-1790s James Watt constructed a small-scale device which made, stored and delivered to a patient what were then called factitious airs or, as we would say today, non-naturally occurring gases. The reason why Watt turned his attention to pneumatic chemistry and medicine was due to the death, on 6 June 1794, of his 15-year-old daughter, Jessy Watt (1779-1794). She had been showing signs of consumption from at least the end of December 1793 when the Derby-based physician Dr Erasmus Darwin (1731-1802) sought to prescribe for her by letter. One of his suggestions was to use the pneumatic therapies that the radical Bristol-based, Oxford- and Edinburgh-trained physician Thomas Beddoes was then developing. Indeed, towards the end of May 1794 at Watt's invitation, Beddoes visited Jessy, to whom he administered various gases, but realised that her case was hopeless.

Watt took the view that in such circumstances, 'the best consolation is to turn the mind to any other subject that can occupy it'. He began, at Beddoes' suggestion, further work on the gas apparatus, writing a short guide to its operation in the form of a letter to Beddoes dated 14 July 1794. This was published in their *Considerations on the Medicinal Use of Factitious Airs, and on the manner of obtaining them in large quantities, parts 1 and 2* (1794). The apparatus was made and sold by Boulton & Watt in various sizes, including portable, but unfortunately no example has been identified, although the possibility exists that one lies miscatalogued in a museum.

Watt's apparatus formed the material core of what Beddoes called the Medical Pneumatic Institution in Bristol. The institution's purpose was to investigate the possible therapeutic effects of gases discovered during the eighteenth century. Watt and other members of his family used their influence in the West Midlands to support Beddoes' extensive fund-raising efforts to establish this institution. It eventually opened in spring 1799 under the superintendence of a young Humphry Davy (1778-1829), a friend of Watt's second son, Gregory (1777-1804), who also showed signs of consumption. Alas neither Beddoes nor Davy could find a cure and Gregory died in 1804 aged 27.

Line drawings of Matthew Boulton and James Watt by Arthur J. Gaskin, 1893.

Watt and Birmingham's Assay Office

Alexandre Parré

Matthew Boulton (1728-1809), who manufactured silver, was instrumental in the establishment of Birmingham's Assay Office in 1773 and one of its first Guardians. Anxious to extend the influence of his business, Boulton likely proposed his business partner James Watt to join the Assay Office. Watt was elected in 1789 to replace the late John Francis, one of the Assay Office's founding Guardians.

The management framework that ruled the Assay Office Birmingham has changed little since its inception. Thirty-six Guardians were responsible for its governance, selected for their standing within Birmingham and the region and for their knowledge of relevant disciplines, including the wrought-plate industries. The early Guardians were drawn from the aristocracy, landed gentry and politics and represented the elite of the town. They generally met once a year and had a duty to ensure the Assay Office was managed in accordance with the 1773 Act of Parliament by which it was founded. Traditionally appointed for life, Guardians had to resign their position if they moved residence more than twenty miles from Birmingham.

From his appointment in 1789 to his death in 1819, James Watt's involvement as a Guardian was sporadic. He certainly attended a meeting on 5 July 1790, signing the minutes for the first time with his characteristic hand. At the same meeting Watt was elected to the more demanding role of a Warden, sharing the role with three others, which committed him to attend assays and taking the Wardens' Oath, promising to abide by Assay rules of conduct and to keep the secrets of the trade. On 4 July 1791, despite failing to attend the meeting, Watt was re-elected as a Warden. However, in 1792, during the Annual General Meeting, which Watt attended, he resigned his wardenship and his post was taken by Boulton's son, Matthew Robinson Boulton (1770-1842).

It is difficult to estimate the influence Watt had in the making of Assay policy or the running of the business. That he found his role as Warden onerous is apparent by his swift resignation. That he maintained his position as a Guardian – albeit as an absentee – is a reflection of the high status of the role.

The centrifugal governor.

The Centrifugal Governor, 1788

Jim Andrew

Watt invented his centrifugal governor to improve the operation of his rotative steam engine. Factory machinery, particularly textile machinery, required a steady speed of rotation from the engine driving it. James Watt's rotative engine was better able to produce a steady speed than its predecessors, but it still slowed down or speeded up if the load was increased or decreased. Watt needed a device which would reduce this tendency to react to a changing load, particularly as the demand for steam-powered machinery grew and factory owners wanted to have multiple machines driven by a single engine. These machines needed to be engaged and disengaged from the drive system without stopping the other machines. A well-established device existed in grain milling, which reacted to speed changes, but this worked by adjusting the gap between the stones rather than altering the speed of rotation.

As Watt's rotative engine became established, control of the engine speed became more important. Watt adapted the centrifugal or ball governor, from grain milling, by modifying it so that a rise or fall in engine speed, with the balls swinging out or falling, reduced or increased the supply of steam to the engine. Changing the steam supply was achieved by a separate valve in the steam supply pipe, often called a throttle valve, and a suitable linkage to the rise and fall of the weights. The modifications were relatively simple and could be added to existing engines by fitting a valve in the supply pipe and driving the ball governor from the engine's output shaft.

Watt's centrifugal governor reduced the variation in speed, that is, the reduction in load would still mean a rise in speed although by less than with an ungoverned engine. In the same way a rise in load would see a small drop in speed. For many industries, this was acceptable, but over time there was a need in some to maintain a constant speed or at least return to the specified speed as soon as possible. This was achieved by various designs of 'feedback governor' where the linkage from the governor to the throttle valve was shortened or lengthened by a device which returned the speed to the specified one.

Page from James Watt's Commonplace Book, n.d. MS 3219/4/171.

Watt's Commonplace Book

Eleanor Beestin

In 1782 James Watt started to keep a commonplace book, a type of personal journal, which was a way of recording thoughts and ideas. Watt's Commonplace Book is a particularly neat, careful and scientific example of what such a book could be. It is very different from other surviving examples: Dr Erasmus Darwin's (1731-1802) Commonplace Book was more of a rough jotter, with quick sketches of ideas for gadgets, machines, and children's toys. Watt's notebook is strictly related to his work: it includes recipes for inks, records of experiments, and designs for furnaces amongst other things, but there is little mention of anything personal, which is true of the majority of Watt's notebooks.

The book shows that Watt was meticulous, and he chose to make this particular notebook especially neat. The handwriting is careful, and the tables are evenly drawn. The drawings have been done with extreme care; on the first page, there are four pictures of furnaces, so beautifully drawn that at first they appear to be printed. Only by looking closely can we see that they were hand-drawn. These drawings show Watt to be not just a scientist, but a proud and meticulous draughtsman.

The notebook itself is large and leather-bound with thick paper; it was an expensive book, bought for this particular purpose. Whilst his other notebooks are also careful and well-kept, his Commonplace Book is even more so. It is neater than his other notebooks, which often contain vague notes, rough jottings, and scraps of paper with quick maths on them. The Commonplace Book even has an index at the back, and a key of scientific symbols at the front. Whilst the exact purpose of the book is unclear, it is possible that he was intending to share it with others, or keep it as a reference guide for himself.

Interestingly, it is only partially finished. Only half of the pages were filled and the rest are blank. Why he gave up on writing his Commonplace Book remains a mystery, but it clearly reveals a lot about him as an individual.

Print from Isaac Taylor, *The Mine*, 1845. Until the development of the steam engine as a provider of rotary motion, horses were used to rotate a winding drum to draw ore, coal or water from mine workings.

James Watt and Horsepower, 1782-8

David Hulse

Horsepower is widely used to rate the power output of an engine. The term was conceived by James Watt between 1782 and 1783 to inform potential customers how many horses would be replaced if they bought one of his engines. Rating the power output of an engine with a horse has been in constant use from these early years of steam power to the present day. Only with the widespread use of standard metric units is horsepower being replaced by kilowatt units.

The first steam engines were used to pump water and the power they produced was unknown as they were used to perform a specific task such as removing water from mines. Once a mine was dry the mine owners expressed little or no interest in how much power was developed. However, with Watt's invention of the double-acting rotative steam engine, work could be undertaken which had previously been carried out by harnessing the power of the horse. Customers naturally wanted to know how many horses these steam engines could replace.

James Watt gave this conundrum careful thought and calculated the amount of work the average horse could carry out in one minute. A prospective customer from Manchester informed Watt that the average mill horse harnessed to a shaft could complete a circle of of 24 feet diameter in a minute, thus rotating the shaft two-and-a-half times. While completing this task the horse was capable of a sustained tension pulling a rope of 172 pounds. By multiplying the distance the horse walked in one minute by this average pull, the universally accepted term foot pounds (lbs/ft.) evolved. The answer to this calculation was 32,400 lbs/ft., which was later increased to 33,000.

Accordingly, the work carried out by one horse is equivalent to the raising of a weight of 33,000 pounds through the height of one foot in one minute. The rating of an engine in horsepower is the work done in one minute by the moving piston divided by the constant number of 33,000. Watt was thus able to inform his customers that they had ten redundant horses if they bought one of his standard engines for a cost of £800.

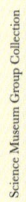

James Watt's model rotary engine.

Model Rotary Engine, 1782

Ben Russell

James Watt's steam engine was a remarkable feat of engineering. It combined into a single machine both new understanding of the nature of heat, and the tacit skills of blacksmiths, carpenters, founders and engine erectors. Pumping engines kept mines clear of flood-water; rotative engines drove new mills, breweries and other industrial concerns. The engine became a potent symbol of Britain's Industrial Revolution.

However, from the start Matthew Boulton (1728-1809) and James Watt also proposed an engine very different from what became their best-known design. Instead of the rotative steam engine, with its reciprocating piston, parallel motion, sun-and-planet gear and flywheel, they planned a rotary engine needing none of these components. Instead, steam would impart motion to a rotor continuously and directly by a process now known as positive displacement. Watt's first thoughts on such an engine came in February 1766, and he prepared a drawing for a 'steam wheel', to be included in his 1769 patent. In Birmingham, Matthew Boulton and Dr William Small (1734-1775) were working on a similar scheme, and their invitation for Watt to join them helped cement his relationship with Boulton, and bring about their celebrated partnership.

In 1782, Watt included the details for three designs of a rotary engine in a patent. Fragments of one of these engines survive inside his workshop. They comprise unfinished brass castings for three hinged vanes around a central rotor, with a port through which to admit steam. The incoming steam would push the vanes around, turning the rotor on its steel shaft, and the vanes would be depressed in turn so that steam could escape out of the engine.

Boulton and Watt were enthusiastic about the project: in 1776, Boulton wrote to Watt how 'If we had a hundred wheels readymade… we could readily dispose of them. Therefore let us make hay while the sun shines…'. However, the technical difficulties of such a design, particularly sealing the vanes to ensure the steam could not simply leak past them, proved insurmountable. The engine was very noisy, and the moving parts would have worn out quickly. Watt's last mention of the idea came in February 1783, by which time his work on the better-known rotative engine was well advanced.

James Watt's model of the sun and planet gear.

The Sun and Planet Gear, 1781

Jim Andrew

The successful application of James Watt's innovations to the pumping engine led to a lucrative and expanding market for Watt and his business partner, Matthew Boulton (1728-1809). However, Boulton wanted to utilise steam technology in other ways, specifically, to drive factory machinery at his Soho Manufactory and asked Watt to develop a rotative engine for this purpose. Watt had seen examples of rotary motion in Newcomen engines and was aware that an improved component was needed to power factory machines. He could see that several different elements would be required to provide a steady rotary motion. These included driving the piston up and down, pushing the beam up as well as pulling it down, converting the beam's movement into rotation, and smoothing the irregular motion of the Newcomen engine with a flywheel, to provide better control of the engine's speed. Solutions for the problems were considered over six or seven years of development. Many different designs were tried and assessed but abandoned as they did not meet Watt's standards.

The sun and planet was Watt's eventual choice for the early rotative engine and he patented the design in 1781. Watt did not use the crank, an established design, probably because it had been recently patented, but also possibly because the sun and planet gear provided all of the elements necessary to produce smooth and efficient rotative power. Although the cost of the most obvious material for flywheels, cast iron, was falling due to improvements in iron manufacture, Watt may have been attracted by an idea which provided regular motion from a lighter and cheaper flywheel. Watt, William Murdock (1754-1839) and other engineers at Soho considered various designs, but the sun and planet gear had the great attraction of doubling the rotational speed of the drive to the flywheel and thus quadrupling its smoothing effect on the engine's output. As more powerful engines were needed, the sun and planet gear's design was limited by the strength of gears inherent in the design. However, by then cast iron was falling in price and the crank patent had lapsed: the sun and planet was thus the preferred choice for powering machinery for about twenty years.

James Watt's portable copying machine.

LETTER-COPY PRESS, 1780

Caroline Archer

Patented in 1780, James Watt's letter-copy press was designed for making copies from a single document. An early 'desktop printer', it was used in offices until typewriters became common. The press answered Watt's need for commercial efficiency and secrecy. It developed from two technological advances: the creation of specialised papers and inks to facilitate the production of multiple copies, and the ability of manufacturers to make smaller, portable versions of larger machines. It also avoided using a clerk to copy sensitive letters and diagrams, which could then be sold to business rivals.

Watt made numerous trials to formulate the paper and ink, to devise a method for wetting the paper, and to make a press suitable for applying the correct pressure to achieve the transfer. The original 'desktop' press was constructed in two forms: a screw-press and rolling-press for office use and a larger version to copy plans and drawings. Later, a more compact, 'laptop' rolling-press was produced, enclosed in a mahogany *secrétaire* for portability.

The letter to be copied was written in special ink and a damp sheet of copying paper was placed over it and a clean sheet of oiled backing paper was laid on top. The package was placed between two felt-covered boards and pressed by a brass roller. This created a 'wrong reading' (mirror image) of the original that soaked through the thin copying paper, and a 'right reading' of the original was discernible on the 'verso' side. When the original was written with sufficient ink, three or four legible copies could be made.

To bring his product to market, Watt formed a partnership with the Birmingham industrialists Matthew Boulton (1728-1809), who provided finance, and James Keir (1735-1820), who managed the business. James Woodmason (d. 1795) was the leading London supplier of Watt's machines, paper and ink. Watt's method of copying letters and drawings was commercially successful and by the end of the first year of business 630 models had been sold. Notable users included Benjamin Franklin (1706-1790), Thomas Jefferson (1743-1826), and Joseph Priestley (1733-1804).

Watt's letter-copy press modernised the office space, accelerated business and ensured confidentiality by giving autonomy of reproduction to the businessman who became both scribe and printer.

Mrs Watts Closet 1791

Set of shelves and deal dresser with drawers
Deal Cupboard with shelves
a small Drugg cupboard
Sugar Cannister a Coffee D°
An open press with shelves
one Long shelf — 1 soap Box 1 Mould Candle Box
1 Kitchen Candle Box 1 Powder Box 1 flour Box
1 Starch Box 1 pattren Box 1 Drugg Box
1 red thread trunk 1 tape D° 1 printing Box
1 Spice Box 1 nail Box
1 hammer & sundry tools
Sundry Stone Jars — D° Glass
Mahoⁿ windlass for thread
2 small china Mortars 2 hair sives
Mahoⁿ tea chest — 3 Cannisters

Entry for Ann Watt's closet from the Heathfield Inventory, 1791. MS 3219/4/238.

ANN WATT (1738-1832)

Kate Croft

James Watt moved from Scotland to England in 1774, after the death of his first wife, Peggy (1736-1773). Two years later, his business partnership with Matthew Boulton (1728-1809) was thriving and their engine business had begun with the installation of an engine at Bloomfield Colliery in Tipton, Staffordshire. In the same year, Watt returned to Scotland, fully intending to arrive back in Birmingham as a married man. The woman Watt intended to marry was Ann MacGregor. Born in 1738 and the daughter of a Glasgow merchant, Ann was intelligent, strong-willed and an excellent domestic manager. Mary Anne Galton (1778-1856) recalled that Ann was so strict regarding household cleanliness that she trained her dogs to wipe their paws before entering the house.

Initially, Ann and Watt enjoyed the same happiness that Watt had experienced with Peggy. Watt wrote to Boulton that marriage to Ann was 'one of the wisest of my actions', and continued, 'I reckon I have made a good [bargain] in securing to myself a valuable friend. All is settled & upon Monday the fatal noose is to be put about my neck, or more emphatically, I am to get a lick of the eternal glue pot.' Although they loved each other, their 43-year long marriage was a difficult one. The separations that Watt's work demanded took their toll, as did Watt's depression, which Ann tried to assuage in various ways. Later, the deaths of their two children, Jessy (1779-1794), who died after a long struggle with consumption, and her elder brother Gregory who was born in 1777 and died in 1804, placed an immense strain on their marriage.

Ann sustained her husband's technical and scientific endeavours, encouraging him through the fluctuations of the Boulton & Watt business and the legal disputes that haunted him. She also supported Watt in his commercial activities. When Watt was away from home, Ann dealt with the constant stream of letters about the steam engine and copy press businesses, communicated with employees, updated Watt regarding customers, other agents and suppliers and offered her advice. Ann outlived her husband by thirteen years and died in 1832, at Heathfield Hall.

On Friday last a Steam Engine constructed upon Mr. Watts's new Principles, was set to Work at Bloomfield Colliery, near Dudley, in the Presence of its Proprietors, Mess. Bentley, Banner, Wallin, and Westley; and a Number of scientific Gentlemen whose Curiosity was excited to see the first Movements of so singular and so powerful a Machine; and whose Expectations were fully gratified by the Excellence of its Performance. The Workmanship of the Whole did not pass unnoticed, nor unadmired. All the Iron Foundry Parts (which are unparalleled for truth) were executed by Mr. Wilkinson; the Condensor, with the Valves, Pistorns, and all the small Work at Soho, by Mr. Harrison, and others; and the Whole was erected by Mr. Perrins, conformable to the Plans and under the Directions of Mr. Watts. From the first Moment of its setting to Work, it made about 14 or 15 Strokes per Minute, and emptied the Engine Pit (which is about 90 Feet deep, and stood 57 Feet high in Water) in less than an Hour. The Gentlemen then adjourned to a Dinner, which was provided in that Neighbourhood, and the Workmen followed their Example. After which, according to Custom, a Name was given to the Machine, viz. PARLIAMENT ENGINE, amidst the Acclamations of a Number of joyous and ingenious Workmen.——This Engine is applied to the working of a Pump 14 Inches and a Half Diameter, which it is capable of doing to the Depth of 300 Feet, or even 360 if wanted; with one fourth of the Fuel that a common Engine would require to produce the same Quantity of Power. The Cylinder is 50 Inches Diameter, and the Length of the Stroke is 7 Feet.——The liberal Spirit shewn by the Proprietors of Bloomfield in ordering this, the first large Engine of the Kind that hath ever been made, and in rejecting a Common One which they had begun to erect, entitle them to the Thanks of the Public; for by this Example the Doubts of the Inexperienced are dispelled, and the Importance and Usefulness of the Invention is finally decided.——These Engines are not worked by the Pressure of the Atmosphere; Their Principles are very different from all others. They were invented by Mr. Watts (late of Glasgow) after many Years Study, and a great Variety of expensive and laborious Experiments; and are now carried into Execution under his and Mr. Boulton's Directions at Boulton and Fothergill's Manufactory near this Town; where they have nearly finished four of them, and have established a Fabrick for them upon so extensive a Plan, as to render them applicable to almost all Purposes where mechanical Power is required, whether great or small, or where the Motion wanted is either rotatory or reciprocating.

The Lord High Chancellor hath appointed Mr. John Cecill, of this Town, a Master in Chancery Extraordinary.

A few Days ago died William Cartwright, a useful hand in the Sword Blade Trade, in the Employment of Mr. Robert Coales; he fell from his Horse as he was returning from his Mother's Funeral.

Newspaper report for the erection of the Boulton & Watt steam engine at Bloomfield, Tipton, 1776.

INSTALLATION OF THE BLOOMFIELD ENGINE IN *ARIS'S GAZETTE* 1776

Kate Croft

On 11 March 1776 Birmingham's *Aris's Gazette* printed an account of a new engine, erected at Bloomfield Colliery in Tipton, Staffordshire, 'conformable to the plans and under the directions of Mr Watt'. For the first time, an account of James Watt's steam engine appeared in the public press. The announcement of the engine's installation in the local newspaper was part of Matthew Boulton (1728-1809) and James Watt's strategy to publicise their new product.

The eighteenth century saw an explosion in printed material. Prior to the 1690s, restrictive Licensing Acts controlled the print trades. By the late seventeenth century, these Acts had lapsed and this, together with the development of new commercial, industrial and residential centres, such as Birmingham, the rise in literacy rates and the emergence of new centres of sociability, such as the coffee-house, the library and clubs, stimulated a demand for a range of reading material. Matthew Boulton had already used newspaper announcements to publicise the products of Boulton & Fothergill and he continued to use these techniques to market the steam engine business.

Boulton and Watt's use of printed material was not restricted to newspapers. Friends and acquaintances helped to publicise their innovations to a wide audience. Dr Erasmus Darwin (1731-1802) wrote about the steam engine in his epic poem, *The Economy of Vegetation*. Stebbing Shaw's (1762-1802) *History and Antiquity of Staffordshire* was a major publication on the history and topography of the county and included an account of the Soho works and the steam engine, also by Darwin. John Robison's (1739-1805) supplement to the 1801 edition of *Encyclopaedia Britannica* included articles on steam and the steam engine, which were revised in later editions by Watt himself. Finally, Boulton and Watt used printed pamphlets during the patent disputes with rival engineers. In these they outlined both the distinctiveness and superiority of Watt's innovations over others, such as Jonathan Hornblower (1753-1815), to retain their legal rights to their patents.

The appearance of the Bloomfield Engine in *Aris's Gazette* demonstrated Boulton and Watt's use of printed material to package and disseminate information about the steam engine to the general public as well as commercial, scientific and technical audiences, an activity which was as innovative as the engine itself.

Soho Manufactory, Handsworth. The image shows the different Boulton & Watt businesses located there, from *Bisset's Magnificent Guide or Grand Copperplate Directory for the Town of Birmingham* (1808). Copper engraving.

LOGAN HENDERSON: ENGINEER FOR BOULTON & WATT

Christopher Olive

When steam engine manufacturing began, James Watt required highly skilled workers. As there were no trained engineers, a diverse range of individuals were employed by Boulton & Watt. One was Logan Henderson who was recruited in 1776. He had been a Lieutenant in the Marines, a sugar planter in Dominica and a land surveyor. He also possessed a love of botany, which is revealed by his letters to Watt describing unusual plants and enclosing pressed flowers obtained whilst he was installing engines. Watt would have related to Henderson's experiences as a surveyor, which required mathematical skills and precision, and his observant mind and interest in the natural world. This meant that he was prepared to support him when others criticised his behaviour.

In July 1780, Henderson was accused by Ann Boulton (1733-1783), Matthew Boulton's wife, of inappropriate behaviour with the women at Soho Manufactory, including keeping a 'handsome housekeeper', known as 'Miss Peggy', as a mistress. Watt wrote on 11 July that he saw no reason 'why your housekeeper ought not to stay in the house though she came as beautiful as Venus,' showing a tolerance of Henderson's sexual misconduct. Watt's concern with 'Miss Peggy' developed only when she ran Henderson into debt in 1782. These debts led to a betrayal of his employers in 1783 when he appealed to the Irish Parliament for payment for erecting the Colclough engine – Watt's patent did not apply in Ireland. Boulton labelled Henderson 'Wasp', presumably as he had 'stung' Boulton & Watt financially, but Watt was still prepared to enter into business with Henderson and granted him a licence to erect a steam engine in 1788.

Watt built up relationships with other workers too. The long-term solution to recruiting skilled engineers was to train apprentices, normally from the age of fourteen, which enabled Watt to educate his workforce and form paternalistic bonds over a long period of time. Two workmen in particular, David 'Davy' Watson and James 'Jammy' Lawson, come into this category.

The treatment of Logan Henderson and other employees challenges the traditional picture of Watt as a dour manager. Clearly, employees were not merely cogs in his machine, but people to whom he related as human beings.

William Murdock by John Graham-Gilbert, early 19th century. Oil painting.

JAMES WATT AND WILLIAM MURDOCK (1754-1839)

Jim Andrew

William Murdoch was born at Auchinleck, Ayrshire in Scotland. After his move to Birmingham in 1777, he changed the spelling of his name to Murdock. His father, John, was a millwright, dealing with machinery for milling and other trades. Murdock seems to have shown enough interest and skill to work with his father and may have visited the Carron Foundry when James Watt was developing his steam engine. In 1777 Murdock travelled south to Birmingham, hoping to see James Watt and obtain employment with Boulton & Watt. Watt was away on business when Murdock called but Matthew Boulton (1728-1809) saw him, heard of his interests and was possibly impressed by a wooden hat which Murdock had machined oval to fit his head.

Murdock became a trusted employee at the Soho Manufactory. He also worked as an engine erector in Scotland and, at Donnington Wood, Shropshire, he converted an engine to the 'expansive working', which was first tested on Watt's canal pumping engine at Smethwick. At this time the partners were spending a significant amount of time in Cornwall, a growing market for the Watt engine pumping water out of local tin mines, and Murdock was asked to relocate there as their resident engineer, a position of responsibility. He stayed in Cornwall for twenty years, but had regular meetings and correspondence with the partners.

Murdock contributed suggestions on engine improvements and became interested in applying steam to vehicles. Watt was unimpressed with the steam vehicle idea, fearing development would take many years to perfect, but he did include the idea in one of his patents, thus protecting Murdock's idea from being copied. More important, Murdock made a major contribution to the development of gas lighting. He lit his own house in Redruth, Cornwall, with gas, and later developed factory lighting into a separate business. He returned to Birmingham in 1798 and was involved in the expansion of the Boulton & Watt business, and the firms which grew out of it. The gas equipment manufacture became a significant activity at Soho and Murdock is considered to be the father of the gas industry.

A Table of Chemical Characters from James Keir, *A Dictionary of Chemistry*, 1771.

JAMES WATT AND JAMES KEIR (1735-1820)

Kristen M. Schranz

James Watt and James Keir met at the Soho Manufactory of Matthew Boulton (1728-1809) in the late 1760s, but it was Dr William Small (1734-1775), a local physician and mutual acquaintance, who fostered the growth of Watt and Keir's early friendship. Keir was born in Stirlingshire and studied medicine at Edinburgh where he befriended Dr Erasmus Darwin (1731-1802). After serving as an army officer – he never practised medicine – Keir settled in the West Midlands where he focused on chemistry and geology, and translated Macquer's *Dictionary of Chemistry* into English. He also leased a glassworks near Stourbridge, Worcestershire, and in 1780 Keir established a huge chemical works in Tipton, Staffordshire, making soda, soap, white and red lead and metal windows.

Watt and Keir co-operated in several ventures. In the 1770s Watt, Keir and Scottish chemist Joseph Black (1728-1799) attempted to decompose sea salt to produce soda. Also known as fossil alkali, soda was a necessary ingredient for the eighteenth-century bleaching, dyeing and soap-making industries. Watt was central to this venture, often sharing Keir's ideas with Black. Although the three men contemplated protecting their process, the scheme was left unrealised. Watt and Keir, however, obtained other patents: in 1779 Keir patented an alloy of copper, zinc and iron (later known as 'Keir's metal'), and in 1780, Watt patented his letter copying press. The copying machine, which duplicated letters and drawings by transferring ink to receptor sheets, necessitated chemical knowledge on several levels. Watt and Keir experimented to find the ideal composition for the ink and paper. Keir advised Watt to increase the amount of gum and tannins in the ink and recommended plain water for wetting the receptor paper. Like Boulton, Keir became a partner in Watt's copying machine business.

In the mid-1780s Watt and Keir gave evidence to the House of Lords concerning the Tools Act. They were against the exportation of industrial machines from Britain to prevent other countries developing new technologies, which could threaten sales of British, especially Birmingham's, manufactured goods. In 1785 both men were elected Fellows of the Royal Society, the leading society dedicated to advancing scientific knowledge. Watt and Keir died one year apart – Watt in 1819 and Keir in 1820.

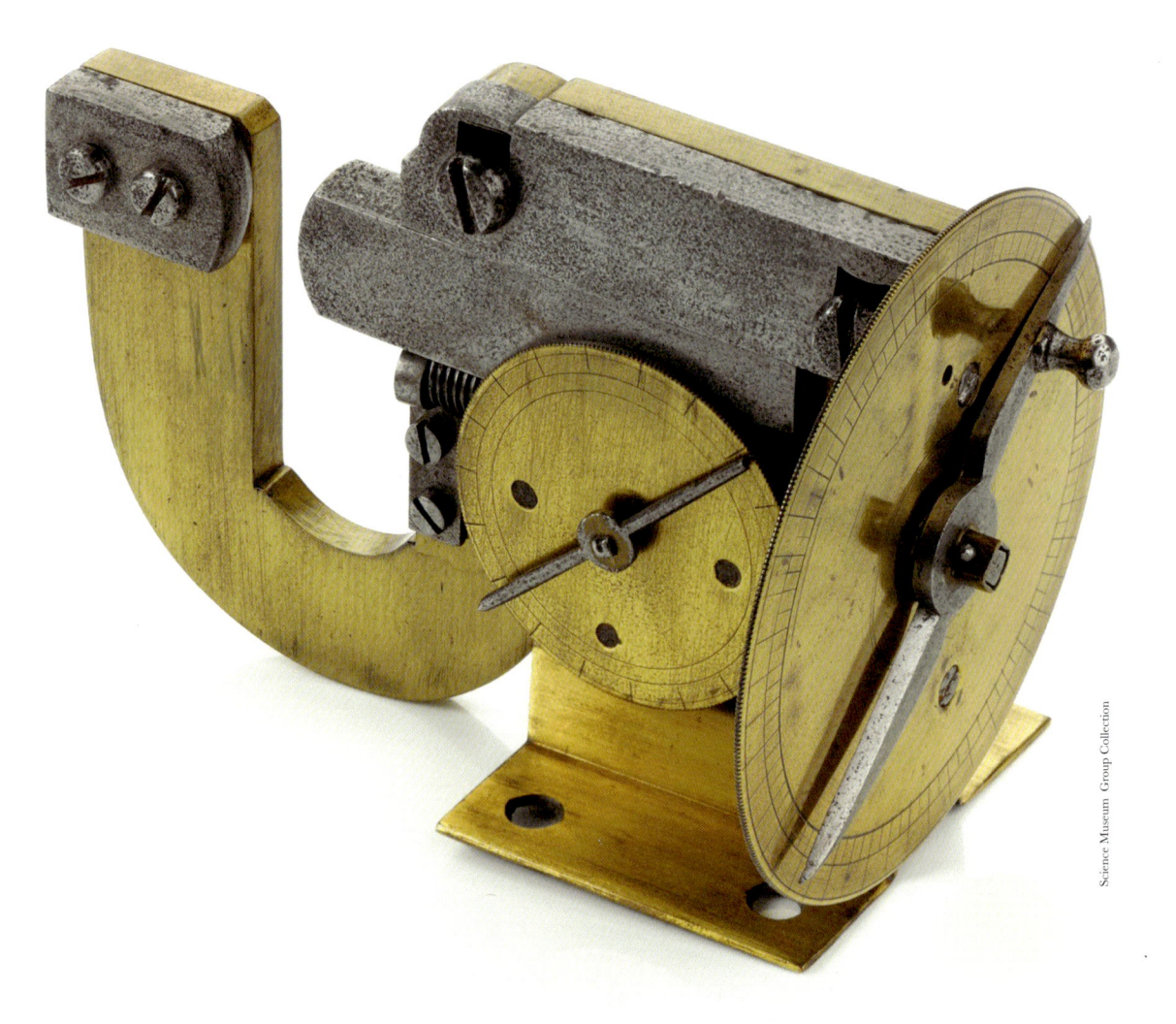

Micrometer. Date unconfirmed.

MICROMETER, 1772

Ben Russell

Making artefacts with increasing precision was a major strand in James Watt's professional life. Starting out as an instrument maker, by 1772 he wrote to Dr William Small (1734-1775) that 'My dividing screw can divide an inch into 1,000 tolerably equal and distinct parts'. The challenge was to apply these levels of attainment to the steam engine. Soon, Watt was able to boast that the engine's cylinders did 'not err the thickness of an old shilling at any part'.

This instrument reflects Watt's interest in precise measurement. It comprised two anvils, one of which can be moved by a fine screw. An object was placed between the two, and the screw was turned so that both anvils gently touched the object. A dial on the front counted the number of turns of the screw, eighteen of which moved the anvil by one inch, and a larger dial on its side divided each rotation into one hundred parts, so that the instrument was theoretically capable of measuring with an accuracy of 1/1800. In so doing, it predated by almost a century the introduction of the engineer's micrometer, a vital part of the profession's toolkit.

However, a note of caution must be sounded over this instrument. It was acquired by the Science Museum in 1876 from James Watt and Co., and there is no accounting for its whereabouts before then. Even H. W. Dickinson in his *James Watt and the Steam Engine* (1927) noted how it embodied some of the concepts that Watt wrote about to his colleagues, 'but so compactly that one would say it was a later production'.

The instrument has some of the hallmarks of objects known to have been made by Watt. Some details are improvised, the quality of the finish is not of the highest, and in practice it does not work as well as intended. There is excessive friction in some parts of its mechanism, and too much variation in others, so it has limited utility as a precision instrument. Rather than having a clear purpose in, for example, engine-building, it may have been a 'proof of concept' model. However, a question mark remains over its creator – James Watt or, possibly, some other young instrument maker.

Erasmus Darwin by Joseph Wright of Derby, 1792. Oil painting.

JAMES WATT AND DR ERASMUS DARWIN (1731-1802)

Kate Croft

Born in Nottinghamshire in 1731, Dr Erasmus Darwin studied medicine at Edinburgh University. He started a lucrative medical practice in Lichfield, Staffordshire in 1756 and pursued his interests in botany, geology, mechanics, climatology and writing poetry. James Watt met Darwin in 1767, when Watt broke his journey back to Scotland from London, to visit Samuel Garbett (1717-1803). Garbett was the business partner of John Roebuck (1718-1794), who was financing Watt's improvements to steam technology. A prominent Birmingham merchant, Garbett introduced Watt to Dr William Small (1734-1775) and Darwin. Watt and Darwin shared a scientific interest in steam. Watt stayed overnight with Darwin and Watt confided the details of the separate condenser to him – evidence of Watt's trust in Darwin. Darwin was also instrumental in persuading Watt to move to Birmingham, enter into partnership with Matthew Boulton (1728-1809), and thus he became a member of the Lunar circle. Watt's correspondence with Darwin, which dates from this point, illuminates their life-long friendship until Darwin's death in 1802.

Darwin supported Watt in his endeavours with steam, encouraging him to continue his efforts in the face of uncertainty. His scientific and technical ability enabled him to converse with Watt about a range of subjects, from the properties of steam, to chemical experiments and mechanical innovations. Darwin also supported Watt on an emotional level. From the start of their friendship, Darwin understood Watt's sensitive nature and responded with his characteristic good-tempered bonhomie. Darwin also advised Watt medically, trying to alleviate the physical symptoms that plagued Watt throughout his life.

Most poignantly, Darwin supported Watt and his second wife, Ann (1738-1832), during the illness of their daughter, Jessy (1779-1794). Jessy suffered from tuberculosis and Darwin suggested treatments. Despite Darwin's efforts, Jessy's condition was fatal and in June 1794, he wrote: 'I do not think I can suggest anything further.' Only a few days later, Darwin wrote again, this time a letter of condolence on the death of Jessy Watt, who had died at the age of 15. He addressed it to 'My dear friend' – Watt was the only member of the Lunar circle to receive this salutation which testifies to the affection that underpinned their friendship.

Matthew Boulton by J. S. C. Schaak, 1770. Oil painting.

James Watt and Matthew Boulton (1728-1809)

Jim Andrew

The partnership between Matthew Boulton and James Watt is often portrayed as that of a skilled businessman, with no technical ability, and an innovative engineer, devoid of business skills. In reality Boulton was a highly competent engineer, as indicated when Watt left him to continue developing the engine, while he spent time in London dealing with the Act of Parliament to extend a patent until 1800. Later Watt remained in Birmingham, running the Soho works while Boulton was in Cornwall, seeking more business and ensuring the correct installation of Watt's modifications. They were, in effect, the ideal partnership between a flamboyant businessman and a careful engineer, each of whom were happy to leave the other to cover his interests while he was elsewhere on business.

Watt first met Boulton in 1768, when he visited Soho on his way back to Scotland from London. Boulton quickly identified the business potential of Watt's improvements to the steam engine and hoped to profit from it by engaging Watt in a partnership to make and market the steam engine design worldwide. Watt's existing partnership with John Roebuck (1718-1794) in Scotland meant that Boulton was only offered a licence to supply engines in the Midlands, which Boulton refused – he had no intention of being second to anyone else in selling power to the world.

Roebuck's eventual bankruptcy brought Boulton the opportunity to become Watt's sole partner and when he bought Roebuck's shares in 1773, the business of Boulton & Watt was born.

Boulton brought not only his wide experience of different Birmingham industries – he petitioned Parliament on their behalf – but also a range of contacts who would help in supplying the components needed for Watt's new design of engine. His engine required much greater accuracy in manufacture than the existing Newcomen steam engine. While Watt often wanted to proceed slowly with his inventions, especially when applying steam power to factories, Boulton pushed ahead, introducing innovations and dealt with problems later.

Despite differences in temperament and personality, Boulton and Watt's business partnership was successful and through Boulton's financial support, Watt was able to make his steam engines high-quality machines which were commercially viable.

Dr William Small by an unknown artist. Line drawing.

James Watt and Dr William Small (1734-1775)

Jim Andrew

Dr William Small was born in Scotland and graduated from Aberdeen University in 1755. Later in 1765 he secured an Aberdeen medical degree. In 1758 he became Professor of Natural Philosophy and Mathematics at William & Mary College, Virginia, introduced curriculum innovations and taught Thomas Jefferson (1743-1826), the third President of the USA. He also became friends with a fellow scientist, Benjamin Franklin (1706-1790). Small, however, suffered from malaria and in 1764 he left for London. Franklin introduced him to Matthew Boulton (1728-1809) and in 1765 Small secured a medical practice in Birmingham, where he became Boulton's doctor and a member of the Lunar Society.

In 1767, after visiting London to deal with his first steam engine patent, Watt called at Birmingham, to visit Boulton's Soho Manufactory, but Boulton was away and he was shown round by Small. Watt eventually met Boulton in 1768, and the three men corresponded primarily about the patent for Watt's separate condenser. Both Small and Boulton had a firm grasp of the technical details of the engine, and made useful contributions to the patent of 1769. Boulton wanted to manufacture the engine but Watt, working with John Roebuck (1718-1794) in Scotland, was happy to continue in the north. One of Small's contributions to the patent debate was to advise against including a drawing of the invention, which Watt had produced. Boulton supported this suggestion and the drawing was not included, just a written description of the innovation. The absence of the drawing had a long-term effect both on the legality of the patent and on the understanding of details of Watt's design.

In 1774, after Roebuck's bankruptcy, Watt moved to Birmingham, welcomed by his friends, including William Small. Sadly, Small died a year later, aged 40, while Watt was in London extending the patent's expiry date to 1800. Small's importance lay not only in his contribution to the steam engine. Like Watt he was interested in many scientific subjects, including geology, chemistry, metals, ceramics, optics (telescopes and microscopes) and clock mechanisms. He also encouraged Watt to publish his findings. Small's early death robbed Watt of an intellectual companion, supporter and collaborator.

PATENT,

JANUARY 5th, 1769,

FOR

A METHOD OF LESSENING THE CONSUMPTION OF STEAM AND FUEL IN FIRE ENGINES.

George the Third, by the Grace of God, &c.

To all to whom these presents shall come, greeting:

Whereas JAMES WATT hath by his Petition h͞bly represented unto us that he hath, after much labour and expense, invented a Method of lessening the Consumption of Steam and Fuel in Fire Engines, which he apprehends will be of great Publick Utility: And in regard he is the first and true Inventor thereof, and the same hath not been practised or used by any other person or persons to his knowledge or belief, he therefore most humbly prayed us to grant unto him, his executors, adm͞ors and assigns, OUR ROYAL LETTERS PATENT under Our Great Seal of Great Britain, for the sole benefit and advantage of his said Invention within that part of Great Britain called England, our Dominion of Wales, and Town of Berwick upon Tweed, and also in our Colonies and Plantations abroad, for the term of Fourteen years, according to the Statute in that case made and provided: WE, being willing to give encouragement to all Arts and Inventions which may be

Front page of James Watt's patent for the separate condenser, January 1769. From 'Specifications of patents for improvements in the steam engine…', f TJ474.

The 1769 Patent

Ian Shearer

James Watt's patent No 913, of 5 January 1769, for his 'New Invented Method of Lessening the Consumption of Steam and Fuel in Fire Engines' secured his best-known innovation – the condensing steam engine – and is among the most significant in the history of technology, energy efficiency, and intellectual property. It provided a fuel-efficient method of solving the problem of cooling resulting from Thomas Newcomen's method of spraying water into the piston chamber to condense the steam and produce a vacuum to enable air pressure to move the piston.

Watt first conceived the separate condenser in 1765, but it took until 1768 to refine the principles, and test the practicalities, enough to define the patent. With the threat of rivals registering the idea first, friends including his then business partner Dr John Roebuck (1718-1794) hastened Watt to London in August 1768 to begin the application. After its approval in early 1769, he finalised the specification, following several drafts, and travelled to Berwick-upon-Tweed, just over the border with England, to witness it on 25 April 1769. Formally enrolled at the Court of Chancery on 29 April, it became the foundation of Watt's eventual success.

The condenser was a Scottish invention and required advanced technical expertise to produce precision-engineered parts. Roebuck's iron works at Carron near Falkirk seemed to provide the necessary skills, but the level of manufacturing precision was not yet sufficiently advanced, and Roebuck's bankruptcy led to a new arrangement. The engine was commercially developed in England after Watt joined Matthew Boulton (1728-1809) in Birmingham in 1774, forming the legendary Boulton & Watt engineering partnership. Led by Watt's initiatives, workers at Boulton's Soho complex developed pumping engines to remove water from mines, and rotative engines to power machinery.

The 1769 patent was the first of several which underpinned the firm's sales. Its initial term was for 14 years, but Boulton strategically succeeded in promoting a Parliamentary Bill in 1775 to extend it until 1800. The monopoly was bitterly resented and challenged by rival engineers over ensuing years, famously leading to litigation in the 1790s, in which Boulton & Watt prevailed. Economic historians have ever since debated the patent's role in helping or hindering steam technology.

Early twentieth-century photograph of James Watt's cottage on the Kinneil Estate, Bo'ness, Scotland.

James Watt's Cottage, Kinneil, c. 1769

Ian Shearer

This former workshop is the only surviving building in Scotland with such a direct link to James Watt. It owes its origins to his connections with Dr John Roebuck (1718-1794), a Sheffield-born doctor, inventor and industrialist. Roebuck pioneered the lead chamber process for making sulphuric acid when he was in business in Birmingham, and moved to Scotland where he established a factory at Prestonpans for manufacturing acid. In 1759 he co-founded the Carron Iron Company near Falkirk, moved to Kinneil and exploited its coal reserves. Pit flooding and the inefficiency of Newcomen pumping engines led him to Watt, who had conceived the separate condenser to improve Newcomen's machine. Roebuck was convinced of the condensing engine's potential and for several years he supported Watt's efforts to turn his invention into a working steam engine.

In November 1768 Watt wrote to Roebuck at his home, Kinneil House, near Bo'ness: 'On considering the engine to be erected with you, I think the best place will be to erect a small house in the glen behind Kinneil.' The adjacent Gil Burn gave water for his experiments. Watt could construct and test his newly-patented separate condenser invention in relative seclusion. There were those such as rival engineer Joseph Hately – also working locally (including for Roebuck) and having patented his own steam engine in 1768 – who were suspected of trying to spy on Watt's more sophisticated designs. Unfortunately, Roebuck went bankrupt in 1773, before a prototype was perfected. Watt, the Kinneil engine, and Roebuck's two-thirds share in the patent, went to Matthew Boulton (1728-1809) in Birmingham where the engine was, at last, commercially manufactured.

Following Watt's departure for Birmingham, the workshop became a wash-house and then fell into disuse. Its unusually steep pantile roof collapsed during the twentieth century and the site became overgrown. More positively, its significance was recognised in 1946, when a cylinder from a local Newcomen pit engine, which Watt had helped to maintain, was erected alongside. Recently, a leading museum curator thought it should become 'an international shrine'. Owned by Falkirk Council, it was A-listed in 2017, when it was also popularly voted among Scotland's top 'Hidden Heritage' sites.

The site represents several aspects of Watt's importance: the dynamics of the relationship between inventor and patron, the trials and setbacks of technological innovation, and the local and national story of the Industrial Revolution.

© by permission of South Lanarkshire Council.

Rutherglen Bridge by Thomas Grant, nineteenth century. Oil painting.

Rutherglen Bridge, 1775

Gordon Masterton

Had James Watt not pursued the conversion of steam into efficient power as his principal passion, he could well have become a leading civil engineer. From 1766 when Watt was 30, until he left Scotland in 1774 to join Matthew Boulton (1728-1809) in Birmingham, he spent more time on civil engineering commissions than he did on his engine. What he achieved in those years, a defining period for most careers, was at least as impressive as any of his civil engineering contemporaries in Scotland and arguably in Great Britain. He certainly earned the respect of John Smeaton (1724-1792), the most eminent civil engineer of the time.

His civil engineering consultancy was grounded in canals and harbours, but he also designed two significant bridges over the River Clyde – one for the Duke of Hamilton and another at Rutherglen. Both were five-span segmental masonry arch bridges but the Rutherglen crossing, being downriver, had longer spans (60ft - 65ft -70ft - 65ft - 60ft).

It was completed in 1775 and gave good service until 1890, when the bed of the Clyde was changed dramatically by the removal of a weir at Glasgow Green. The bridge was 16ft wide between parapets and surviving photographs show its elegant simplicity, with robust piers and cutwaters, and lightness in the arches. The roadway is close to the arch extrados (upper curve) to minimise weight, and Watt's original drawings reveal hidden weight-saving measures – local voiding above the piers and hollow spandrels (spaces between one side of the arch's outer curve and the ceiling), created by two internal longitudinal walls surmounted by pointed arches, thus minimising rubble infill. This was probably inspired by Smeaton's design for Perth Bridge (1771).

In the days before steam hammers drove long piles down to bedrock, the muddy bottom of the Clyde had to be accommodated by founding the piers on fir platforms 3ft below the river bed, with 56 9-inch-diameter iron-shod piles hammered down 8ft below. Real horse power raised the heavy weights that delivered the final blows. Each array of piles was protected by a skirt of timber sheet piling driven down 6ft. These measures showed that Watt understood risks and paid attention to detail: the mark of a thoughtful, principled engineer.

Science Museum Group Collection

James Watt's surveyor's compass.

WATT'S SURVEYOR'S COMPASS, c. 1767-1773

Ben Russell

For part of his career James Watt worked as a surveyor. He started in 1767, in partnership with the engineer Robert Mackell (d. 1779) to improve Glasgow's links to the Firths of Clyde and Forth. There then followed a pause while Watt finished his work on the steam engine's separate condenser. But in October 1769, he began a series of surveys that would occupy him until the autumn of 1773.

Watt had previously made and sold surveying instruments. However, he needed his own and acquired this fine surveyor's compass, made by George Adams the Elder (1709-1772). The compass would have been used in conjunction with a tripod, one of which survives inside Watt's workshop at the Science Museum, London. With the compass mounted on the tripod, Watt would have peered through its sights to spot distant landmarks and measure the angle between them, gradually plotting the lie of the land. The compass's inscription, '…to His Royal Highness the PRINCE of WALES', suggests a manufacturing date between 1756, when Adams began in the instrument trade, and 1760, when the Prince of Wales became King George III. Given that this predates Watt's surveying projects, it is likely that he acquired the compass second-hand at a later date.

Watt's surveys have been underplayed, but they taught him valuable skills for his work on engines: for example, how to estimate the cost of structures and to cope with the politics and personalities that these projects entailed. Through his surveys Watt also made contact with the engineer John Smeaton (1724-1792), of whose 'countenance and friendship' he was proud. Historian L. T. C. Rolt believed that Watt would have ranked with the great canal engineers James Brindley, John Rennie and Thomas Telford had he continued in the field.

However, surveying also revealed Watt's diffidence. He wrote how, 'Nothing is more contrary to my disposition than bustling and bargaining…', and that, 'I would rather face a loaded cannon than settle an account or make a bargain'. The compass represents Watt at a tipping point in his career, moving on to new projects, but also questioning his own ability to succeed.

Postcard showing a tin-glazed punchbowl made for the Saracen's Head Inn around 1760 by the Delftfield Pottery Co.

The Delftfield Pottery, 1768

Ben Russell

During the late 1760s, James Watt experienced a remarkable diversification in his business interests. The steam engine was just one of several projects running simultaneously: Watt was a shopkeeper, proto-engineer, surveyor – and a potter. Glasgow's Delftfield Pottery was established in 1748, operating from a site close to the central Broomielaw Quay. Its original product was Delftware, soft, liable to crack and scratch easily, and its popularity was waning. Watt was appointed in February 1768 as technical advisor, to turn the company's fortunes around. Doing so ultimately meant turning production over to earthenwares, the traditional British ceramic ware.

Before that stage was reached, Watt had numerous experiments to undertake. In 1768 he tried to replicate stoneware and porcelain manufacture; some of the containers surviving in his workshop have recipes for soft paste porcelain written on their lids. There are also samples in the workshop of cobalt, lead oxide and manganese, vital ingredients for glazes. An entire drawer is filled with test firings of cream-coloured clay, accompanied by Watt's notes that they were fired 'by 55 degrees', and 'by 80 degrees' of 'Wedgwood's thermometer'.

In his work for Delftfield, Watt was isolated from the main centres of pottery production in England, and he complained that his 'insulated manufactory has much to struggle with'. The quality of its products was also not very high. He wrote in 1772 that, '…we make damned bad ware', and a selection of misfired rejects appeared in his workshop as chemical storage containers. But his long-term expectations were positive. He wrote to his friend Dr William Small (1734-1775) in January 1769: 'Our pottery is doing tolerably', and although he was 'sick of the people I have to do with', he thought the business 'will turn out a very good one'. The company built a solid reputation making and exporting cream-coloured wares.

Watt's work at Delftfield was important in two ways. It gave him a steady income just when his growing family needed it. In the longer term, the chemical work required for the pottery, and the study of heat's effects in its kilns, provided an important theoretical underpinning for his understanding of the steam engine.

Peggy had been some days in an unusual way but was better, on wednesday night she had taken her pains & was exceeding ill all day, was delivered of a dead child by Mr Hamilton at seven o'clock at night & appeared easy after it, but restless which encreased upon her, untill a cold sweat foretold her approaching fate with her latest breath she begg'd her friends to comfort me & died without a groan In her I lost the comfort of my life a dear friend and a faithfull wife, may she enjoy that happiness in another state she wanted in this life of sorrow we were married upon the 16th of July 1764 & she died the 24th of Sepr 1773 — She bore me 4 living children, 2 sons & 2 daughters & died of the 3d son who was buried with her of these children a son & daughter are left me whom god long preserve

Entry for 29 September 1773 from James Watt's Notebook, MS 3219/4/135.

MARGARET (PEGGY) WATT (1736-1773)

Kate Croft

In 1764, at the age of 28, James Watt decided to marry. His wife was his cousin, Margaret Miller, known as Peggy and there had long been 'an early and constant attachment' between them. Peggy's 'sweetness of temper and lively, cheerful disposition' had a positive effect on Watt, who was prone to despondency and low spirits. At this time, Watt was an instrument maker and merchant in Glasgow. During his marriage to Peggy, Watt developed the separate condenser. She was a constant practical and emotional support to Watt throughout the years when his steam engine innovations were far from certain to succeed. Peggy wrote to him in 1768: 'I beg you would not make yourself uneasy though things should not succeed to your wish, if it will not something else will, never despair.'

Watt's surveying commissions, and later his work at Kinneil House for John Roebuck (1718-1794), led to regular separations from Peggy. During these periods, Peggy managed the shop and acted as point of contact between Watt and his surveying business clients. But both felt the pain of his absence from home, especially when Peggy was pregnant, as she was in 1767, when Watt wrote to her: 'Oh Peggy, I wish I was with thee even for a day or two.' They had five children, but only two survived into adulthood. John was born in 1765 and died the same year. Margaret was born in 1767 and James junior in 1769. A second daughter, Agnes was born in 1770 but died in 1772.

In 1773, during one of Watt's absences, Peggy was pregnant with their fifth child. After receiving a letter from his cousin, Robert Muirhead, warning him that she was dangerously ill, Watt immediately set out for home, but Peggy and her child had died on Friday 24 September, the day Muirhead had written his letter.

Watt was devastated by Peggy's death and recorded in his notebook his final tribute to her: 'In her I lost the comfort of my life, a dear friend and a faithful wife.' Watt's early achievements owe a great deal to his relationship with his first wife.

Model Newcomen Engine repaired by James Watt at Glasgow University.

MODEL NEWCOMEN ENGINE

Nicky Reeves

In 1756 the 20-year-old James Watt was employed by Robert Dick junior (1722-1757), Professor of Natural Philosophy at the University of Glasgow, to repair some astronomical instruments bequeathed to the institution by Scottish-born Jamaican plantation-owner, slave-owner and astronomer Alexander Macfarlane (1702-1755). This led Watt to establish a workshop in the University's premises on the High Street. He styled himself 'Mathematical Instrument Maker to the University', and through his work he became connected to a vibrant community of academic experimenters and theorists including John Anderson (1726-1796), Joseph Black (1728-1799) and John Robison (1739-1805).

The University's model Newcomen steam engine was one of approximately 100 instruments and devices stored in the 'Experiment Room & Closet', which were used for teaching and experimenting. It may have been manufactured by either Jeremiah Sisson (1720-1783/4) or his father, Jonathan Sisson (1690?-1747), but this remains conjectural. In the winter of 1763-4 Watt was asked by Anderson to repair the model, which had repeatedly proved troublesome. Watt later recalled that at first, 'I set about repairing it as a mere mechanician', but soon realised that significant design improvements could be made, which were informed by the latest theories of heat. It was whilst attempting to repair the model that Watt realised in 1765 that a great deal of heat was wasted in the condensation process. The result was his first key innovation in steam engine technology, the separate condenser.

Although there is no evidence that Watt ever attached a separate condenser to this specific model engine, it remains a pivotal object. Small fragments of model steam engines developed in Watt's Glasgow workshop on Trongate from this period survive, including what is thought to be the first model separate condenser, most of which was salvaged from Watt's later Birmingham workshop in his house at Heathfield, Handsworth, by the Science Museum in the 1920s, having lain largely untouched following Watt's death in 1819. They are currently on long-term display in the recreated workshop in that museum. Nevertheless, these are only fragments, and the model in the Hunterian at the University of Glasgow is almost certainly the only surviving complete or nearly complete model engine worked on by Watt in that period.

(First Quadrangle)
OLD UNIVERSITY, GLASGOW

Lithograph of the Old University, Glasgow. Undated.

Watt and the University of Glasgow

Stephen Mullen

Between 1753 and 1774, James Watt was a resident of Glasgow, originally a medieval market town situated on the banks of the River Clyde and home to a cathedral and university. During the eighteenth century, the influx of wealth accumulated by colonial merchants – who specialised in the import of slave-grown tobacco, sugar and cotton – transformed the town into a bustling commercial city. For almost all of that 21-year period, Watt was associated with the University of Glasgow – then known as Old College – and the institution was instrumental in Watt's rise. Old College – the spiritual home of the Scottish Enlightenment – was then located on Glasgow's High Street, a hub of ideas and activities where famous philosophers such as Adam Smith (1723-1790) mixed freely in clubs, literary societies and taverns with colonial merchants. This environment ignited the embryonic career of the great inventor who became a driving force of the Industrial Revolution.

After his mother's death in 1753, Watt moved to Glasgow to be trained by his uncle – his mother's brother – in the mercantile trades. Opportunities were few, and he travelled to London in 1755 to be trained as a mathematical instrument maker. Returning to Glasgow in September 1756, Watt connected with Old College staff initially through Professor George Muirhead (1715-1773), another kinsman of his mother, and he became close friends with Professors Robert Dick junior (1722-1757) and James Moor (1712-1779). Recognising Watt's expertise in repairing instruments, the latter two professors invited Watt to fix items bequeathed to Old College by Jamaican slave-owner and Old College alumnus Alexander MacFarlane (1702-1755). These instruments – a mural arch, a meridian transit, an astronomical sector, a clock, globes, micrometers and telescopes – were subsequently gifted to and formed the establishment of Old College Observatory. Watt was paid £5 sterling in December 1756 on completing the task – perhaps his first paid employment in a new trade – and was afterwards appointed mathematical instrument maker to the University.

This period evolved into a highly successful career with key phases: making instruments, developing steam engines and latterly working as a civil engineer before he made his way in Birmingham in 1774.

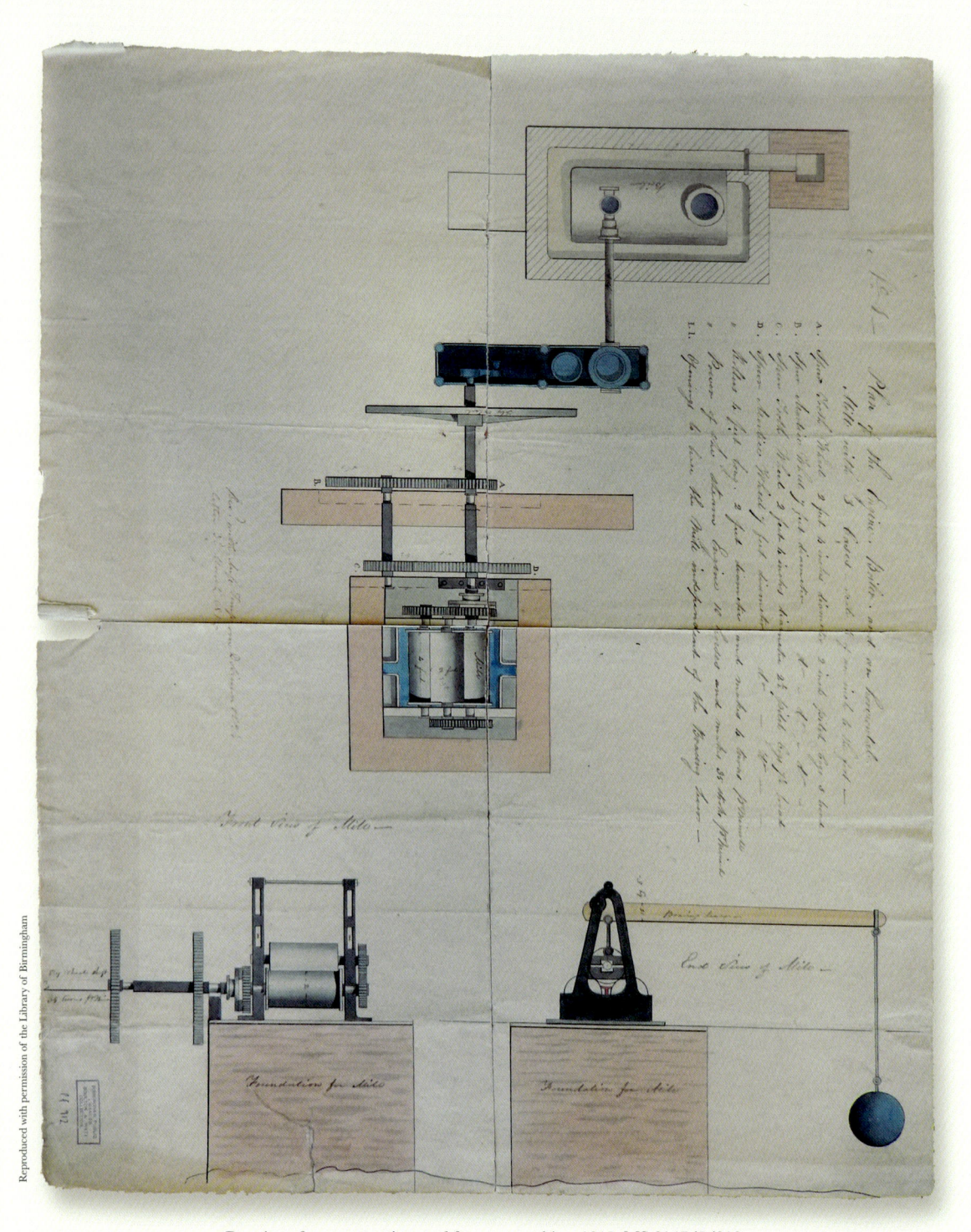

Drawing of a steam engine used for cane crushing. 1815, MS 3147/5/912.

Transatlantic Slavery and Commerce

Stephen Mullen

James Watt's family were heavily involved in transatlantic commerce, including trading in enslaved persons. His father, James Watt senior (1699-1782), was a merchant in Greenock using agents to trade in sugar and tobacco with North America and the Caribbean from 1733 until 1771. In the early 1740s, he sent grain and corn to Antigua via Archibald Cochran, in return for sugar, rum and cotton. James Watt's brother, John, joined the business and branched into slave-trading. On 17 March 1762, Walter McAdam 'received from John Watt a Black Boy which I promise to deliver to Mr John Warrand Mercht in Glasgow'. The enslaved boy, Frederick, clothed in breeches, a waist-coat, a black cravat, shoes and a blue coat, eventually became the property of James Brodie, the chief of Clan Brodie. The Watt family were at the centre of the Atlantic trading network in Greenock and Glasgow for over forty years.

James Watt also profited from the trade. He acted as a mercantile agent for his father in 1753-4, whilst he was in London in 1755-6 and in Glasgow following his return in 1756. He was also a major shareholder in Delftfield Pottery from 1764 until his death (his initial investment of £240 increased twenty-fold in that period). Early nineteenth-century shipments of delft left the Clyde destined for, amongst other places, Antigua, Trinidad, Jamaica and Grenada, islands with large contingents of resident Scottish planters. In contrast, on 31 October 1791 James Watt wrote: 'We heartily pray that the system of slavery so disgraceful to humanity were abolished by prudent though progressive measures.' The extent of Watt's awareness of a personal contradiction – that he was complicit with and benefited from slavery, whilst also expressing abolitionist sentiment – remains unknown.

Between 1800 and 1830, Caribbean slave plantation owners were the main overseas customers and source of profits for Boulton & Watt steam engines, which were used to crush sugar cane prior to the boiling of sugar syrup. Selling steam engines to the Caribbean was, however, not undertaken by Watt himself. In the late 1790s, alongside his business partner, Matthew Boulton (1728-1809), he retired and the business was managed by their sons, James Watt junior (1769-1848) and Matthew Robinson Boulton (1770-1842).

James Watt, father of the inventor by an unknown artist. Unsigned and undated. Oil painting.

JAMES WATT OF GREENOCK (1699-1782), FATHER OF THE INVENTOR

Valerie Boa

This unsigned painting of James Watt of Greenock, the father of James Watt, appears to be a close copy of a family portrait by an unknown artist. James, the younger son of Thomas Watt (*c.* 1642-1734), was born on 28 January 1699 and is said to have served an apprenticeship to a builder and shipwright in Cartsdyke prior to settling in Greenock. The father of the famous engineer had a successful business career encompassing several commercial activities, including participation in the slave trade. He was also prominent in community affairs as a member of Greenock Town Council for over twenty years and, as Treasurer for much of that time, he took an active and informed interest in town developments. James Watt married Agnes Muirhead (1701-1753), but they suffered the losses of three children in infancy and only their sons James and his younger brother John (1739-1762) lived into adulthood. John, however, lost his life at sea at the age of 23 while travelling to America on one of his father's ships.

Young James did not have a robust constitution and was home-schooled during his early years by his well-educated and cultivated mother. When he first attended school he did not prosper either academically or socially until he moved to the local grammar school at the age of 13 when he began to make particular progress in mathematics. Watt also spent time in his father's workshop making models and repairing ships' instruments. He developed a craftsman's skills and his aptitude for these delicate tasks was such that the workmen would say of him, 'Jamie has gotten a fortune at his fingers' ends'. This hands-on training in practical applications stood him in good stead in later life when he was trying to translate scientific theories into physical reality.

Agnes died in 1753 and her husband's heavy commercial losses reduced the fortune he had built up through years of industry and effort. Instead of working in his father's business, James was sent to Glasgow in 1753 to live with an uncle and enhance his commercial skills, a move which widened his contacts and extended his intellectual horizons.

Thomas Watt, grandfather of the inventor by an unknown artist. Unsigned and undated. Oil painting.

Thomas Watt (c. 1642-1734), James Watt's Grandfather

Valerie Boa

The date and artist of this portrait of Thomas Watt are unknown, but it may have been commissioned by his son or grandson from an earlier image or images which do not survive. Thomas's origins were in Aberdeenshire, where his father, according to his grandson's manuscript, 'Of my Parentage', had been a small landowner. His father, probably a strict Protestant, was, however, killed during the religious conflicts of the Civil War in the 1640s. The land was lost and he was left destitute. An uncle who was a blacksmith took him into his care and when he reached a suitable age he was apprenticed to a carpenter and stonemason. Once Thomas had served his time he came to Glasgow and developed a talent for the mathematical sciences, but he could not find suitable teachers. He moved to Ireland and entered the service of a clergyman; part of the arrangement was that he would benefit from instruction by his master. This early grounding appears to have been successful and Thomas is documented as a student at Aberdeen University in 1668.

By 1683 Thomas Watt is recorded at Cartsdyke near Greenock where he became a teacher of navigation. He prospered and held important community roles, including serving as Bailie of the Barony of Greenock and church elder and treasurer of the west parish of the town. He married Margaret Shearer (1651-1734) and they had six children, three of whom died in infancy followed by their daughter at eighteen years of age. Their two surviving sons were John (1694-1737), who became a surveyor, and James (1699-1782), father of the engineer. James Watt, the subject of this book, was later to sell a published version of his Uncle John's 1734 *Survey of the River Clyde* at his shop in the College of Glasgow.

Thomas Watt died in 1734 and his gravestone recorded him as 'Profesor of the Mathematicks'. He died before the birth of his grandson in 1736, but James clearly respected his grandfather's memory and benefited from studying Thomas's books and papers on navigation and mathematics, which were passed down through the family. Thomas provided his grandson with his birthplace and upbringing in a prosperous, commercial town and with an intellectual legacy in practical science.

McLean Museum and Art Gallery, Inverclyde Council.

A View of Greenock, 1768 by Robert Paul. Engraving.

A View of Greenock in 1768 by Robert Paul

Valerie Boa

This print of Greenock on the River Clyde in 1768 is the earliest known view of the town where James Watt was born in 1736. The artist was Robert Paul (1739-1770), who studied at Glasgow's Foulis Academy and created engravings and topographical works of the lower Clyde area. Paul succeeded in capturing the energy and bustle of Greenock as a port. The prominent church near the harbour, known as the Mid Kirk, was opened in 1761 with seating arrangements planned by James Watt's father, but the spire was not completed until 1787. James Watt's father, also James Watt (1699-1782), was an energetic entrepreneur who worked as a shipwright, ship-chandler, builder and merchant. His son was born in William Street, which runs from the harbour to the Mid Kirk.

Greenock originated as a herring fishing village. Its prosperity as a town can be traced to the growth of this trade in the early eighteenth century. In 1707 the townspeople built a state-of-the-art harbour which was completed in 1710. Paul's image shows the circular form of the East and West Quay along with a tongue called the Mid Quay.

The flourishing herring fishing trade led John Scott to found Scotts' Shipbuilders in 1711, which initially built herring busses and other small craft. New trading ventures required the construction of more ambitious vessels and Greenock's first square-rigged sailing ship, the brig *Greenock*, was built by Peter Love in the 1760s. Up until the American Revolution in 1775 most of the large vessels trading to the Clyde had been built in America but the ensuing disruption boosted local shipbuilding. Sea-going vessels were unable to reach Glasgow until the deepening of the River Clyde which started in 1774, so nearby Greenock and Port Glasgow on the Clyde Estuary were ideally placed to take advantage of international trading opportunities. One of the cargoes imported was to dominate Greenock's fortunes, along with shipbuilding, for centuries. Sugar grown in slave plantations in the West Indies was brought to Greenock and the town's first sugar refinery was opened around 1765 in Sugarhouse Lane. Greenock's prosperity was partially due to its participation in the transatlantic slave trade.

reassess the man, his context and his legacy. Watt was clearly an important Scottish inventor, a West Midlands entrepreneur and innovator, a participant in Enlightenment thinking and activity and an individual whose influence extended beyond Greenock, Glasgow, Handsworth and Birmingham to the wider world. If we are going to understand him in the twenty-first century, we need to see him as a man of his times, a contributor to the Scottish Enlightenment, a participant in the West Midlands industrial environment, an artisan who required support from others, and a son, husband and father, whose family helped to create and cement his achievements. Watt is not only an icon whose light shines into the present; he was a complex individual whose life experiences and legacies illuminate a world of invention, innovation and reputation.

Notes

[1] *The Annual Biography and Obituary for the Year 1819*, Vol 3 (London: Longman, Hurst, Rees, Orme and Brown, 1819), p. 391.

[2] Thomas Carlyle, 'A Mechanical Age', *Edinburgh Review*, 1829.

[3] Peter M. Jones, *Industrial Enlightenment: Science, Technology and Culture in Birmingham and the West Midlands 1760-1820* (Manchester: Manchester University Press, 2008).

[4] Malcolm Dick, 'The West Midlands in War and Peace', in Andrew Watts and Emma Tyler (eds), *Fortunes of War: the West Midlands at the Time of Waterloo* (Alcester: West Midlands History Limited, 2015), p. 7.

[5] Library of Birmingham, Archives and Collections, James Watt Papers, MS3219/4/62/7, James Watt to William Small, n.d., *c.*1773.

[6] William Small to James Watt, 8 October 1773 in James P. Muirhead, *The Origin and Progress of the Mechanical Inventions of James Watt*, Vol 2 (London: John Murray, 1854), p. 63.

[7] James Boswell, *The Life of Samuel Johnson LLD* (London: George Routledge and Sons, 1867), p. 252.

[8] Library of Birmingham, Archives and Collections, James Watt Papers, MS3219/4/5/1/56, Ann Watt to James Watt, 25 December 1786.

[9] Erasmus Darwin, *The Botanic Garden, A Poem in Two Parts, The Economy of Vegetation and The Loves of the Plants* (London: Joseph Johnson, 1791), Canto 1, lines 259-288.

[10] Samuel Smiles, *Lives of Boulton and Watt, Principally from the Original Soho MSS* (London: John Murray, 1865), p. 269.

James Watt and the steam kettle, print by James Scott after a painting by Marcus Stone (1840-1921), *c.* 1884. Steel engraving.

Watt and the kettle continued to be pervasive after his death. As a boy, he was allegedly inspired to study steam whilst watching vapour condense on a spoon. This incident was romanticised in books and images during the nineteenth century and beyond.

Watt's impact was global as well as national. One example is that his name was applied internationally as a unit for measuring power after 1908. His influence permeated throughout Japan in the late nineteenth century and in the 1930s, both the Japanese Government and the James Watt Society of Japan celebrated the man as an inventor. The 200th anniversary of Watt's birth resulted in a major exhibition in Tokyo in 1936 to celebrate his technological importance. In the western world, his image was used in adverts to sell products as diverse as whisky and electrical machines. Watt became a secular icon disembodied from his time and place.

The 200th anniversary of James Watt's death provides an opportunity in 2019 to visitors. Though Matthew Boulton and James Watt were heavily involved in establishing the foundry, by 1800 they had retired. Their sons, Matthew Robinson Boulton and James Watt junior took over the management of the businesses created by their fathers in earlier decades, including the foundry itself.

Remembering Watt

Matthew Boulton predeceased his partner by ten years. Despite Watt's fragile health and frequent illnesses, psychosomatic or otherwise, he lived longer than most of his Lunar colleagues and died on 25 August 1819 at the age of 83. One of his earliest biographers, Samuel Smiles, commented on Watt's longevity: 'the creaking gate hangs long on its hinges',[10] he wrote. Watt devoted his final years to continued invention and innovation. He developed a heating system for the new Hunterian Museum at Glasgow University but he also experimented at his home in Heathfield, Handsworth in his workshop which has been preserved at the Science Museum, London as a remarkable cornucopia of Watt's interests in many scientific and technical projects. Scholars are still investigating the workshop to throw light on Watt's interests in subjects as diverse as musical instruments and optics.

Watt's death was not the end of Watt. His one surviving son, James Watt junior, pursued a filial project to preserve and promote his father's reputation. The firm of Boulton & Watt flourished under the management of Matthew Robinson Boulton and James Watt junior, selling steam engines to pump water out of coal, tin and copper mines, to power textile machinery and to crush cane on Caribbean sugar plantations. However, James Watt junior was not just a successful businessman. In the early 1790s his radicalism and support for the French Revolution achieved notoriety, including a public verbal assault by Edmund Burke MP, which alienated him from his father for a while. They were reconciled, however, and James junior became a successful businessman continuing his father's commercial legacy.

After his father's death James Watt junior vigorously projected his father's scientific and engineering achievements into a wider world. James Watt was honoured in medals, memorialised in statues, celebrated in books and venerated in paintings and prints, some of which are illustrated in the articles in this publication. Our image of Watt as an inventive genius stems substantially from the work of his son. The myth of

The Soho Foundry in 1895, photographed immediately after closure.

recorded in the Archives of Soho in the Library of Birmingham as major contributors. Translating ideas into reality was a collective enterprise in the late eighteenth and early nineteenth centuries. Relevant high-quality skills were also in short supply and the solution was to train apprentices, who also appear in the archival record.

As the sales of steam engines became increasingly important to the business, the Soho Manufactory proved to be inadequate to the task of manufacturing the products. A new factory was built in Smethwick, Staffordshire, in the mid-1790s, a few miles away from the Soho Manufactory and well-served by the local canal network, specifically to make steam engines for a burgeoning market at home and abroad. The Soho Foundry, as it became known, was completed in 1796: it was the first custom-built structure for making steam engines and therefore marks the beginning of the mechanical engineering industry in the United Kingdom. Much of the building survives but it requires considerable investment to preserve the structure and make it accessible to

> Gale after gale, He crowds the struggling wind;
> The imprison'd storms through brazen nostrils roar,
> Fan the white flame, and fuse the sparkling ore.
> Here high in air the rising stream He pours
> To clay-built cisterns, or to lead-lined towers;
> Fresh through a thousand pipes the wave distils,
> And thirsty cities drink the exuberant rills.–
> There the vast mill-stone with inebriate whirl
> On trembling floors his forceful fingers twirl.
> Whose flinty teeth the golden harvests grind,
> Feast without blood! and nourish human-kind.
> Now his hard hands on Mona's rifted crest,
> Bosom'd in rock, her azure ores arrest;
> With iron lips his rapid rollers seize
> The lengthening bars, in thin expansion squeeze;
> Descending screws with ponderous fly-wheels wound
> The tawny plates, the new medallions round;
> Hard dyes of steel the cupreous circles cramp,
> And with quick fall his massy hammers stamp.
> The Harp, the Lily and the Lion join,
> And GEORGE and BRITAIN guard the sterling coin.[9]

Darwin's verse not only vividly outlined the steam engine's penetration into economic and social life, it also revealed that Watt's engines had become part of popular culture to initiate a new age of steam.

As the steam engine business grew, Watt and Boulton needed the assistance of engineers and skilled workers to translate ideas into reality. William Murdock was an important assistant who began to work for Boulton & Watt in 1770 and upon whom Watt relied heavily. He was also an innovator in his own right in developing steam technology in new directions. Unlike Watt he believed that steam engines could be used to power locomotives, and he was a pioneer in the use of gas as a fuel. There were other engineers, including Logan Henderson, who are less well-known, but are

The Triumph of Steam

James Watt's domestic circumstances were crucial in enabling him to operate successfully as a businessman and inventor. As well as steam engine improvements to the pumping and rotative engines, which various articles in this book describe, Watt's inventive mind focused on other developments, such as the copying machine of 1780: the world's first commercial copier. Its development revealed Watt's painstaking approach to technological innovation, his business acumen and also his concern to prevent disloyal clerks from selling his ideas to other businesses. The machine enabled Watt to copy private letters and diagrams without requiring others to reproduce important documents by hand. The machine was made at the Soho Manufactory in Handsworth and marketed widely. James Keir, another Scottish member of the Lunar Society, played a major role in developing the machine as a commercial project. Watt always patented his inventions. Whether this helped in promoting innovation or preventing improvements by others is a subject of debate amongst historians.

Watt's closest Lunar colleague was Erasmus Darwin, who shared his ideas with Watt and unlike his friend, did not patent his inventions. Darwin served Watt in at least one other way. He celebrated Boulton & Watt's steam engine in print. In Part 1 of his best-selling poem, *The Botanic Garden* (1791), Darwin personified the engine as a multi-purpose awe-inspiring force which wrenched ore from the earth, worked bellows in forges, pumped water into towns, ground grain into flour, dragged copper from the mines of Anglesey (Mona) and stamped copper coins with King George III's head in the Soho Mint:

> Press'd by the ponderous air the Piston falls
> Resistless, sliding through its iron walls;
> Quick moves the balanced beam, of giant-birth,
> Wields his large limbs, and nodding shakes the earth.
> The Giant-Power from earth's remotest caves
> Lifts with strong arm her dark reluctant waves;
> Each cavern'd rock, and hidden den explores,
> Drags her dark coals, and digs her shining ores.–
> Next, in close cells of ribbed oak confined,

However, this steam engine marked a turning point in the development of their business partnership. The significance was summed up by Boulton, in his well-known statement to James Boswell in 1776: 'I sell here, sir, what all the world desires to have – POWER.'[7] The Boulton & Watt business continued to develop. Its fluctuations included money worries, patent disputes, problems with employees, and disagreements with customers, most notably those from the Cornish market.

Watt's personal life took a new direction in 1776, when he returned to Scotland and came back a married man. Watt's second wife was Ann MacGregor, the daughter of a Glaswegian linen manufacturer, with whom Watt had done business in the past. Watt's children, Margaret and James junior, also left Scotland to complete the new family. Watt and Ann's marriage lasted until his death in 1819 and while they shared a great deal of affection for one another, it was not always a happy one. Ann was proud of her husband and the reputation he had acquired as the improver of the steam engine. The pressures of the business led to long periods of time away from each other and took their toll on their marriage. Equally as detrimental was the pain they suffered due to the illnesses of both the children they shared. Gregory, a bright, sensitive and talented boy, was born in 1777 and Janet, known as Jessy, was born in 1779. Jessy contracted tuberculosis and died at the age of 15. Gregory, who was an accomplished artist and geologist, also sickened with the disease and died at the age of 27 in 1804. Both Watt and Ann were devastated by the deaths of their two children.

Ann's excellent organisational skills were also put to use in the service of Watt's business activities. In a world where the letter was the most important means of communication, especially in business, Ann received letters at Harper's Hill – their first home – and Heathfield, and either sent them to Watt himself, who was frequently absent in Cornwall or Scotland, or forwarded them to Boulton or the appropriate contact at Soho. Ann was the person to whom employees applied if Boulton and Watt were unable to be contacted, and she ventured to Soho on occasion to pass on letters, collect others and cast her eye over the activities there. 'I now think my dear James you know as much of your business as you would have done were you at home,'[8] she wrote to him in 1786, a clear indication that as much as James Watt's professional success was achieved with the help of many men, it was also the result of significant help from both his wives.

Birmingham: the Workshop of the World

The motivation for Watt finally deciding to move to Birmingham in 1774 was the loss of his wife, Peggy, in childbirth in 1773. Watt was devastated. His naturally melancholic temperament had been balanced by Peggy's cheerful and gentle personality. She had supported him and he was bereft after her death, as well as now being the sole parent to two young children. Suddenly, he no longer had reason to stay in his native country. He left his children, Margaret, aged six, and James junior, aged four, in the care of his relatives and moved to the West Midlands.

Watt's move to Birmingham enabled both his business partnership with Boulton and his personal friendships with the Lunar men to flourish. Unfortunately, William Small, the quiet, unassuming and engaging doctor who exercised a calmly diplomatic influence on the more flamboyant Lunar friends, died in 1775. For Watt, Small was instrumental in providing advice for the patent that Watt took out in 1769 for the steam condenser and was a constant support over the steam engine trials. More poignantly, Small had consoled Watt over the death of Peggy and to him Watt confided some of his most heartfelt emotions at her loss. 'I know that grief has its period; but I have much to suffer first,'[5] Watt wrote to Small in 1773, to which Small replied: 'I most deeply condole with you, and wish I could comfort you also … Come to me as soon as you can.'[6]

Life continued, however, and now resident in Birmingham, Watt could begin work on tackling the problems inherent in the engine that had been brought down from Kinneil. In the course of trying to get the engine to work, he and Boulton ordered a new cylinder from John Wilkinson, an iron-master working at Coalbrookdale and brother of Mary Priestley, the wife of Joseph Priestley. Fanatical about iron and thus nicknamed 'Iron-Mad', Wilkinson had patented a new boring machine that created cylinders which were smoother along their internal circumference, which vastly improved the ability of Watt's engine to perform efficiently. In March 1776, the first Boulton & Watt-produced engine, manufactured to Watt's improved design and with a cylinder supplied by John Wilkinson, was erected to pump water from the Bloomfield Colliery at Tipton.

Orders for the new engine arrived soon after news of this new form of mechanical power filtered out from Tipton. In Cornwall copper and tin mining became both a fertile market for Boulton & Watt's engines and a source of professional irritation.

of his mechanical processes. Both Small and Darwin were intellectually interested in the subject. With Watt's arrival at Soho, the Birmingham-based cohort found an engineer with the talent and scientific imagination to provide the answer they had been seeking, while Watt found a group of men equally enthused by technical innovation and scientific endeavour. The network that formed between them was the basis of the growing Lunar circle and over the next few years, Boulton and Small tried to entice Watt to relocate to Birmingham. But Watt was settled in Scotland and so was his wife, with their friends and family close by, and Watt had a reasonable means of supporting them, even if his first steam engine lay in disconnected pieces at Kinneil. But he returned to his innovations in between his surveying work and by 1768 he had a second engine with which he was able to make trials and convince Roebuck to continue his financial support by becoming a two-thirds shareholder in the invention. Watt applied for a patent to secure his innovations in his own name. He returned to London for this purpose and again, on his way back home, he visited Boulton and Soho. Boulton was as convinced as Roebuck of the potential of Watt's innovations and increasingly tried to convince Watt to move south. Watt was tempted, especially as his relationship with Roebuck was becoming strained.

Despite Boulton's faith in him, Watt's faith in himself and his engine was waning. The patent 'for a new method of lessening the consumption of steam and fuel in fire engines' was granted in January 1769 and he returned to Kinneil to begin work on a full-scale engine. But it proved frustrating, while conversely, his work as a surveyor continued to be more abundant and profitable and in 1770 he was appointed as surveyor for the Monkland Canal. To the dismay of Small and Roebuck, canals then dominated Watt's life for the next four years. Just when it appeared as if he would never return to his engine project, the Scottish bank, Neale, James, Fordyce and Down collapsed, the repercussions of which were to be the bankruptcy of Watt's financial backer, Roebuck. Boulton, who had invested money in Watt's engine, became one of Roebuck's creditors and offered to buy out his share of the engine and in May 1773, Roebuck agreed. Boulton became the majority shareholder in Watt's engine and was tantalisingly close to becoming Watt's business partner in practice as well as in name. But Watt still had no intention of moving south.

Watt gained another supporter in his efforts to improve the steam engine, again through his contacts at Glasgow University. His model had, eventually, given proof of concept, but the next step was a full-scale engine. His friend Joseph Black knew the entrepreneur and industrialist, John Roebuck, who had recently leased the estate of the Duke of Hamilton at Kinneil, near Bo'ness on the south bank of the Firth of Forth and was working the lucrative collieries and saltworks in the locality. Roebuck's Newcomen engines could not drain his mines fast enough, but Black saw that Watt's prototype engine could provide the answer – it gave Roebuck the technical solution he wanted and Watt the financial backing he needed. The partnership between Roebuck and Watt also gave Watt the space he required, in the form of a workshop in the grounds of Kinneil House, where the first full-scale engine was made. The nearby Carron ironworks at Falkirk also promised to provide the skills in casting iron for engine parts. But the process was arduous and frustrating and Watt's other business interests were pressing in on him. His partner in the merchant's shop, John Craig, died in 1766 and Watt had to repay the capital he owed to Craig's heirs at a time when he needed to support his growing family. This meant that, by 1766, the steam engine project was shelved, and Watt had to step away from his mechanical and scientific explorations. By the mid-1760s he was no longer working at the University, his shop on Trongate was sold and he set up as a surveyor working on Scotland's growing canal network.

Watt's work on Scottish canals introduced him to his future Lunar Society friends in England. In 1767, while working as joint surveyor of the route between the Forth and the Clyde, he visited London to promote the Bill needed to authorise it. On his return to Scotland, he visited Birmingham to meet Roebuck's business partner, Samuel Garbett. Watt's stay in Birmingham included a visit to the Soho Manufactory of Garbett's good friend and fellow industrialist, Matthew Boulton. Boulton was absent when Watt arrived, but another friend, William Small, offered to show Watt around. On the same visit, Watt also met Erasmus Darwin and stayed with him at Lichfield. The friendship between Watt and the Midlands Lunar men was instant.

The key to the bond that was forged between the four men was steam. Boulton had investigated the possibility of using steam-powered pumping engines at his huge Soho Manufactory to increase the flow of water through waterwheels which powered some

James Watt Cottage, Kinneil with, in front, an iron boiler from a Newcomen engine. Modern photograph by Ian Shearer.

Savery. According to Watt's own recollection, inspiration struck him on a Sunday afternoon in the spring of 1765 when, strolling through College Green, the notion of the separate condenser occurred to him. By the following day he had begun working on a model of his innovative idea.

Alongside his intellectual tussles with the problems of steam technology, he also developed his business interests, by becoming part-owner of the Delftfield Pottery Company and going into partnership with John Craig in 1759, setting up a workshop, initially in Glasgow's Saltmarket and then on Trongate to make and sell mathematical instruments. Watt's personal life changed with his marriage to his cousin Margaret Miller, known as Peggy, in 1764. Marriage to Peggy brought a degree of stability to Watt's life. Peggy was a loyal and constant support, helping Watt with the merchant business, bearing five children, raising the two who survived infancy and encouraging him in his steam engine endeavours.

Greenock, but he had well-placed family connections there. Watt's first stay in Glasgow was of relatively short duration.

At Glasgow University, Watt met Robert Dick junior, Professor of Natural Philosophy (Science). Dick clearly recognised Watt's abilities and, seeing that Glasgow was not going to help him achieve his potential, encouraged Watt to leave Scotland for London. With a recommendation letter from Dick and his father's blessing, Watt, together with his friend John Marr, set off for London in 1755. Despite Dick's letter of introduction, Watt failed to secure a master, due to the rigid restrictions of the guild that regulated all aspects of his intended trade, the Worshipful Company of Clock-makers. Eventually Watt did gain the training he required, packing four years' worth of training into one and by 1756 he was back in Scotland. On a business trip to Glasgow on behalf of his father, Watt again encountered Dick, who asked him to repair some astronomical instruments that had been bequeathed to the University. Thus began Watt's tenure at the University of Glasgow. In 1759 Watt gained the title of Mathematical Instrument Maker to the University, a post he held until 1764, residing in his own shop in the quadrangle. Watt's connection with the University, however, continued until his death and not only through his personal contacts. He later endowed prizes for students who excelled in scientific subjects and in the twentieth century, the University created a James Watt Professorship in Electrical Engineering and named a building after him.

Moving Forward: Scottish Experiments

One of the main benefits of Watt's time in Glasgow was the relationship that he developed with two other academics, Joseph Black and John Robison. Despite the disparity in their backgrounds and status, Watt, Black and Robison became close friends. Watt benefited from the connection as Black and Robison broadened his intellectual horizons and their discussions encouraged him to consider subjects beyond the purely mechanical. It was through Robison that Watt began to turn his attention to the steam engine, when Robison asked Watt to help him make a working model of a steam engine running on wheels. Their attempt was unsuccessful, but in 1760 another Glasgow University associate and friend, John Anderson, asked Watt to repair a model Newcomen engine. Thus began Watt's adventures in steam. Throughout the next five years he grappled with the principles of steam, latent heat and the mechanics of Newcomen's design, while reading as much about the subject as he could, from Papin to

Trongate, Glasgow. Location of James Watt's business where he made and sold mathematical instruments in the 1760s. Print. From Samuel Smiles, *Lives of Boulton and Watt* (London: John Murray, 1865).

him to follow his early inclinations towards mathematics, engineering and reading. His father encouraged him by supplying his son with a miniature workshop, complete with workbench, tools and a forge. He learnt as a child how to make, mend, invent and solve problems, in the physical environment of his child's workshop.

Watt's early propensity for mechanics prompted him, as he approached adulthood, to set his course towards life as an instrument-maker. In 1753, he was seventeen years old and left Greenock for Glasgow, in pursuit of this goal. His decision was precipitated by two significant changes in his family's fortunes. In that year his mother, Agnes, died and his father's businesses began to experience difficulties. Glasgow was the natural destination for the young James Watt. Not only was the university city growing in size and wealth, due to the same trading ships that imported and exported goods along the Clyde to industries – banking, insurance and retailing – were both producers and consumers of the vast array of goods that could be purchased from high streets and markets throughout the country. These varied influences were instrumental in Watt's technical and scientific development. They played a part in shaping his environment, his education and training, his business and professional partnerships, and the outlets for his products, which would, in turn, shape the age that followed.

Since his death Watt has been celebrated as a genius who improved the steam engine, but his innovations were the product, not of one man working alone, but of a complex network of individuals – other intellectuals, engineers, skilled workers and also members of his family – who supported his undeniable talents. Watt was also constantly improving the efficiency of the steam engine, as well as being responsible for other inventions, such as the copying machine – again a product where others played their part. Watt's interests were wide and reflected the contemporary curiosity in scientific, mechanical and philosophical subjects. He was an entrepreneur, but he remained an artisan, a maker and a tinkerer, spending his last days in the same kind of space where he spent his childhood years, the place he felt most at home – his workshop at Heathfield Hall in Handsworth, near Birmingham.

From Greenock to Glasgow

James Watt was born in January 1736 to James Watt senior and Agnes in Greenock, a port near Glasgow on the River Clyde. James was their eldest surviving child. His brother, John, was born in 1739 but died young, at sea, in 1762. Watt's mother was from a long-established Greenock family, the Muirheads. Agnes was a sensible, capable, refined woman. She was intelligent, knowledgeable and an excellent domestic manager. However, the loss of three children in infancy would have been hard to bear and Agnes lavished care and attention on James, to protect his fragile health.

James Watt senior was a merchant, trading in the goods that made Greenock a vital port to the Scottish economy – salt, coal, herring and imported sugar from the slave plantation islands of the West Indies. His son's childhood was a combination of ill health and instruments, which set the young Watt on the path he ultimately took as an adult. Of delicate health and indulged by his worried mother, his formal schooling was sporadic. Watt was an intelligent and enquiring child, and his time at home allowed

View of the Bullring, Birmingham after William Hollins (1763-1843), *c.* 1830-1840. Japanned iron tray.

non-incorporated status, which meant it was not restricted by trade guilds and attracted dissenters, who were barred from public and military life by the restrictive Clarendon Codes, to come and thrive in trade and industry. Birmingham had a culture of innovation: more patents were taken out in the town prior to 1850 than anywhere else in the country, other than London. It is not without some justification that the West Midlands can be termed the 'Silicon Valley' of the eighteenth century.[4]

The Britain that helped to shape Watt was a nation rich in natural resources which underpinned its growing manufacturing base. It had an elite, which saw the economic potential of investment in artisans and engineers, and ambitious men took every practical and educational opportunity to improve themselves and become generators of new industry. It had international trading routes and markets and a navy that protected the passage of people and goods. The workers in mines, workshops, factories and service belt and the middling ranks of Protestant merchants who were growing in wealth and influence were no longer looking north for their economic future, but to England in the south. With the Jacobite uprising only ten years behind them, it was to their larger neighbour that they looked for stability and prosperity. Glasgow University reflected that progressive pragmatism and the ideals of the Enlightenment. Clubs such as the Political Economy Club brought merchants and academics together and men such as John Anderson, Professor of Natural Philosophy, offered general lectures on the application of science to industry, and visited the artisans of the town in their workshops. Others including David Hume and Adam Smith produced works of philosophical and economic importance, reflecting the growth of Enlightenment ideals and the political economy that connected with the Industrial Revolution. Across Scotland, into England, and outwards to Europe and America, networks were formed, and lines of communication opened, facilitated by the growth of the publishing and printing trades and the dissemination of knowledge in printed form, together with a rise in personal letter-writing, education and literacy.

It was through those networks that Watt came into contact with the Lunar men of the Midlands and while Birmingham did not have the same formal academic credentials as Glasgow – it did not have a university – it had a similar progressive and pragmatic spirit, embodied in men such as Matthew Boulton. Birmingham also had a strong tradition of self-help, informal and useful learning, of which the Lunar Society was only one well-known example. The town also had many practical advantages that attracted men like Watt. It was known as the city of a thousand trades and the toyshop of Europe. It had many skilled metalworkers producing small decorative objects, known as toys, predominantly buttons, but ranging far beyond this from buckles to vinaigrettes. It was also famous for its production of intricate machines, including locks, guns and machine tools. John Baskerville's innovations contributed as well to Birmingham's emergence as the main centre of the British printing industry outside London. When Watt moved to the town in 1774, it had easy access to vital raw materials, such as coal and iron ore, in nearby South Staffordshire. The town had excellent transport links. First there were turnpike roads but from the 1760s canals snaked from Birmingham to the Black Country, Bristol, Hull and Liverpool and coaches also ran regularly to and from London and the north. It also benefited from its towns. Watt was witness to much of this. Only nine years after Watt's birth, the Jacobite leader, Bonnie Prince Charlie led his troops from the Scottish Highlands and captured Edinburgh. Watt's father's workshop in Greenock was searched by soldiers pursuing Bonnie Prince Charlie. Later, in 1791, a Birmingham mob rioted, destroying the homes of many associated with non-conformism and political reform. The tinder spark had been Joseph Priestley's radicalism and a dinner to mark the anniversary of the storming of the Bastille. While Watt stayed away from political or social radicalism – he was a conservative man – and was unscathed by the Birmingham Riots, the events to which he was witness exemplified the tumultuousness that could suddenly engulf people, even in a century of relative stability. Despite the existence of unrest, domestic stability allowed for men like Watt to apply their mind and skills to the scientific and technological challenges of the day and invest in the future.

Glasgow and Birmingham

One of the reasons Watt and others like him were able to respond to those challenges was the free flow of information and knowledge between 'savants' and 'fabricants',[3] or thinkers and doers. This was especially true in the two locations of most significance to Watt. In both Glasgow and Birmingham, new knowledge was shared between the new breed of Enlightenment academic, such as Joseph Black, and the artisans who had developed a range of skills over generations. The public lecture was a key means of disseminating scientific, technological and philosophical knowledge to new audiences. Watt's workshop at Glasgow University became a hub for staff and students to meet and discuss new ideas. Later, in Birmingham, Boulton's Soho House and Darwin's Lichfield home acted in much the same way. Although of different ranks socially, university-educated professors and doctors associated with apprenticeship-trained engineers, surveyors and skilled workmen and each learnt from the other. Watt engaged in both worlds.

Like Birmingham, mid-eighteenth-century Glasgow was a rapidly developing town. Burgeoning with new wealth that made its way from Greenock, which acted as Glasgow's port until 1775 when the River Clyde became more easily navigable for trading vessels, Glasgow was the most significant town in lowland Scotland. The linen industry had been its most important trade, but the ships from Britain's colonies imported tobacco and other goods, including sugar. By the 1750s, the Scottish central moved away from the land to the growing towns and manufacturing districts and became tradespeople, labourers and skilled workers.

The social hierarchy remained powerful enough to require the lower and middling ranks to learn the language of civility and politeness in order to reap the rewards of patronage, but fluid enough to allow for the possibility of social mobility and ambition. Many landowners invested old money in the innovations of skilled artisans, who could, and did, become wealthy with new money. Coal joined wool as one of the country's most significant products, fuelling new mechanised forms of power. Trading routes opened up between Britain and overseas and goods flowed between them. Investment in the mercantile infrastructures, such as ships, harbours and ports, supported international commerce.

The wealth that was generated by this growth in trade poured into the built environment, the developing urban areas, not just London, but towns such as Birmingham, Bristol, Glasgow and Liverpool, as well as the stately homes and parks of the elite. It also found its way into the pockets of the wider public. Not everyone benefited, but an increasing number and proportion of the so-called lower orders found that they had expendable income. This wealth was used to purchase the goods produced by entrepreneurs, including Watt's associates in the Lunar Society. Ceramics made at Etruria by Josiah Wedgwood, toys and silverware from Matthew Boulton's Soho Manufactory, soap from James Keir's Tipton chemical works and the books written by Thomas Day, Joseph Priestley and Dr Erasmus Darwin all signalled the rise of the consumer. Yet much of the wealth that benefited the majority was generated on the backs of the enslaved – tea, tobacco, sugar, rum, cotton – were the products of slave communities, including the plantations of the Caribbean and North America. Due to its Parliamentary form of government, British patriots saw the country as one of the freest countries in the world, but much of its wealth was predicated on the enslavement of millions of people.

The eighteenth century was a period of relative domestic peace and yet it saw the final bloody incarnation of Jacobite nationalism, to restore the Stuart dynasty, culminating in the 1745 Rebellion. The War of Independence between 1775 and 1783 saw the loss of the American colonies and dealt a blow to the belief that Britain was invincible. Popular disturbances, including food riots, were frequent in both countryside and

John Pinkerton, *Map of the British Isles* (England, Scotland, Ireland), 1818.

designed and executed – he was, after all, a craftsman at heart. Though he could become despondent and cast down by the trials of life, he was excited by scientific enquiry. 'I can think of nothing but this Machine', he wrote to the surgeon, James Lind in 1765. Later, in 1770, he explained to William Small, that even though he had taken work on a canal building project, 'at the same time I resolved not to drop the engine, but to prosecute it the first time I could spare.'

In spite of the battles he fought externally, such as with the Cornish mine owners in the patents dispute, or internally with his own depression, Watt did not give up. Tenacity and uncertainty were a curious mix in his character, which did not always sit easily alongside his scientific and technical capabilities and his importance as an innovator. By re-evaluating James Watt the inventor, alongside James Watt the man, his achievements become more, rather than less impressive.

The scientific and technical accomplishments of James Watt are well documented, but he is more than merely 'the great improver of the steam engine' and his successes with steam technology need to be considered in light of his other achievements, as well as his legacy as one of the major players in the eighteenth-century Industrial Revolution.

Scotland and England in the Time of Watt

For Watt, the age in which he reached adulthood and lived was a fortuitous one. In the mid-eighteenth century, Britain emerged as a powerful industrial nation, in which scientists (or natural philosophers) grew in confidence and popularity, inventors and engineers developed new technology to tame nature and increase manual productivity. At the same time, traditional deference to Church and King was threatened by a new individualism and belief in self-realisation and progress. Britain was changing and became a politically unified nation. The Act of Union between Scotland and England in 1707 brought both countries together under one government and stimulated the integration of their economies.

The agricultural revolution increased the quantity of food and enabled enabled a greater proportion of the populace to participate in a market economy, though many were impoverished by enclosure. Industrial and commercial developments stimulated urbanisation, transport and the expansion of mining. Significant numbers of people much longer, at least as a man of business. I cannot help being dispirited, because I find my head fail me much; business is an excessive burden to me, and little prospect of any speedy release from it.' The most succinct summary of these traits in James Watt's character is given by Watt himself in 1803: 'I was never endowed with the speedy decision, firmness of character, and intrepidity necessary for a public station.'

This, however, is only part of the story. Despite his disappointments and worries, Watt's powerful mind made him intellectually curious, an evident trait while he was still a child, and which continued to motivate him to undertake practical, problem-solving challenges in his workshop at Heathfield during his retirement years. He was a true polymath.

Despite his own claims to natural inactivity, as a young man, growing up in the Scottish port of Greenock, Watt was ambitious, hard-working and a fast learner. His move to London was predicated on his wish to learn the skill of instrument-making, and he completed a one-year course of training that enabled him to return to Scotland and gain employment in the trade. In Glasgow, his ambition to better himself was revealed through the friendships he enjoyed and the networks in which he moved. 'Our conversations then, besides the usual subjects with young men, turned principally on literary topics, religions, belles-lettres, &c; and to those conversations my mind owed its first bias towards such subjects, I never having attended a college, and being then but a mechanic', he later wrote. He may have thought himself 'but a mechanic', but his talents, enthusiasm and hard work brought him into the orbit of others who shared his interests and encouraged his professional endeavours. John Robison recalled that 'his [Watt's] own high relish for these things [mathematics and mechanics] made him pleased with the Chat of any person who had the same tastes as himself.'

Watt was clearly sociable and his rooms at Glasgow University became a meeting place for young students of scientific inclination, leading to Watt's request for a dozen china tea cups, a tea pot and a sugar box from his father. He became a valued member of the Midlands Lunar Society who amongst other things, according to Erasmus Darwin, indulged in 'a little philosophical laughing'. This suggests that through the misanthropic gloom, the light of humour, warmth, conviviality and friendship could shine.

Watt's caution, although an irritant to those with whom he worked, was a reflection of his need for perfection, to ensure all the elements of his innovation were orderly, well-

Interior of the first Hunterian Museum with statue of James Watt by William Stewart (1823 - 1906), undated. Oil on canvas.
Remembering Watt: two artisans and Francis Leggatt Chantrey's statue.

transformed social, commercial and cultural life throughout the eighteenth and nineteenth centuries and provided power to change the world. Watt did not invent steam power, but he dramatically enhanced the efficiency of Thomas Newcomen's pumping engine and developed the sun and planet gear to turn the up-and-down pumping mechanism into a circular motion. This last innovation transformed traditional manual trades by applying steam power to the factory system.

Much has been written about Watt. There are celebratory accounts, popular surveys, detailed biographies and academic studies. *The Power to Change the World: James Watt (1736-1819) – A Life in 50 Objects* is different. It illuminates the life and legacy of James Watt through an exploration of places, people and things. We are locating him in his geographical and intellectual contexts, paying due attention to his family and friendships. The book also considers how he has been remembered and represented since his death. It is designed for a wide audience but underpinned by knowledge and research to inform, enlighten and entertain.

Character and Personality

While James Watt has come to represent the ambitious, go-getting spirit of the Industrial Revolution, the man himself was more complex. Endowed with great intellectual abilities and practical skills, he was often unsure of himself and vulnerable to slights and disappointments. 'Even his powerful mind sank occasionally into misanthropic gloom', observed his cousin, Jane Campbell, while John Robison recalled that Watt was 'modest, timid, easily frightened by rubs and misgivings, and too apt to despond'. His health was a constant concern to him. He suffered from migraines, stomach complaints and low spirits and openly referred to his 'natural inactivity and want of health and resolution'. Watt was cautious, preferring to take the development of his initial innovation, the separate condenser, slowly and was unwilling to risk the financial stability of his young family by sacrificing paid, if mundane, employment as a surveyor, for the sake of his experimental engine at Kinneil. His restraint exasperated others: 'You are letting the most active part of your life insensibly glide away', John Roebuck told him in 1768: 'A Day, a Moment ought not to be lost.'

He found commercial activity burdensome and detrimental to his health. In 1785, he wrote to Matthew Boulton: 'My own health is so bad that I do not think I can hold out

INTRODUCTION

Malcolm Dick and Kate Croft

James Watt died at his home, Heathfield Hall, in Handsworth, Staffordshire, on 25 August 1819 and he was interred locally in St Mary's Parish Church. Watt was born, educated and developed his steam engine in Scotland where he benefited from the fertile intellectual and economic opportunities provided in Greenock, Glasgow and Kinneil. However, the friendships, skills and opportunities he encountered in Birmingham and the English West Midlands enabled his ideas to be improved and translated into commercial commodities. Both Scotland and the Birmingham area can claim Watt as one of their own and this book has benefited from the involvement of Watt scholars and heritage professionals in Scotland and Birmingham as well as in London and elsewhere. Like Watt's innovations, this has been a truly collaborative project.

James Watt was both shaped by, and shaped, the age in which he lived. When he died, he was celebrated as 'the great improver of the steam engine, and one of the most eminent mechanical philosophers, if not the most eminent, of modern times'.[1] Steam engines ushered in the 'Age of Machinery'. Writing in 1829, Thomas Carlyle announced the all-encompassing role of steam technology:

> On every hand, the living artisan is driven from his workshop, to make room for a speedier, inanimate one. The shuttle drops from the fingers of the weaver, and falls into iron fingers that ply it faster. The sailor furls his sail, and lays down his oar; and bids a strong, unwearied servant, on vaporous wings, bear him through the waters.

Steam's impact was global as well as national:

> Men have crossed oceans by steam; the Birmingham Fire-king has visited the fabulous East....There is no end to machinery. Even the horse is stripped of his harness, and finds a fleet firehorse yoked in his stead…. We remove mountains, and make seas our smooth highway; nothing can resist us. We war with rude Nature; and, by our resistless engines, come off always victorious, and loaded with spoils.[2]

Watt is synonymous with the steam engine. It became a potent symbol of the Industrial Revolution, the period of immense economic, technological and scientific change that

Contents

1   Introduction

25   50 Objects and Articles

125   Acknowledgements

126   Timeline

128   Archives

129   Museums, Art Galleries and Heritage Sites

132   Contributors

133   Further Reading

Published by West Midlands History Limited
Minerva Mill Innovation Centre, Alcester, Warwickshire, UK.
© 2019 West Midlands History Limited.
© All images are copyright as credited.

The rights of contributors to be identified as editors and authors of this work have been asserted by them in accordance with the Copyright, Designs and Patents Act 1988.
Editors: Malcolm Dick and Kate Croft

All rights reserved. No part of this publication may be reproduced, stored in a retrieval system, or transmitted, in any form or by any means, electronic, mechanical, photocopying, recording, or otherwise, without the prior permission of West Midlands History Limited. This book is sold subject to the condition that it shall not, by way of trade or otherwise, be lent, re-sold, hired or otherwise circulated without the publisher's prior consent in any form of binding or cover other than that in which it is published and without a similar condition including this condition being imposed on the subsequent purchaser.

ISBN: 978-1-905036-56-1

Cover image: *James Watt sitting beside a drawing of a rotative beam engine*, Carl Fredrik von Breda, 1792.
© Science & Society Picture Library.

Caric Press Limited, Merthyr Tydfil, Wales.

The Power to Change the World

James Watt (1736-1819)
A Life in 50 Objects

Edited by Malcolm Dick and Kate Croft